Movement and Dance
in Early Childhood

All titles are available from Paul Chapman Publishing
http://www/paulchapmanpublishing.co.uk

The 0–8 series

The 0–8 series edited by Professor Tina Bruce, deals with essential themes in early childhood which concern practitioners, parents and children. In a practical and accessible way, the series sets out a holistic approach to work with young children, families and their communities. It is evidence based, drawing on theory and research. The books are designed for use by early years practitioners, and those on professional development courses, and initial teacher education courses covering the age-range 0–8.

Movement and Dance
in Early Childhood

Second Edition

Mollie Davies

P·C·P
Paul Chapman
Publishing

Paul Chapman Publishing
A SAGE Publications Company
6 Bonhill Street
London EC2A 4PU

SAGE Publications Inc
2455 Teller Road
Thousand Oaks, California 91320

SAGE Publications India Pvt Ltd
B-42, Panchsheel Enclave
Post Box 4109
New Delhi 100 017

Library of Congress Control Number: 2002108316

A catalogue record for this book is available from the British Library

ISBN 0 7619 4053 7
ISBN 0 7619 4054 5 (pbk)

Typeset by Dorwyn Ltd, Rowlands Castle, Hants
Printed and bound by The Cromwell Press, Trowbridge

To Mary Wilkinson, dear friend and colleague, whose wisdom, patience and care guided me through the first edition and whose memory has sustained me through the second.

Contents

Preface

Dr Mollie Davies holds an international reputation for her outstanding and scholarly work in the field of Movement and Dance Education. She has influenced many adults and young people with whom she has worked and her contribution has been honoured with an MBE for services to dance education and by a fellowship from the Royal Academy of Dance.

The examples in this unique and ground-breaking book on movement and dance development from birth to eight years show her love of children and a depth of knowledge and practical experience in helping them to become skilled, creative and imaginative in a wide range of movement-oriented activities. She helps early childhood educators and parents in very practical ways and yet her guidance is always rooted in a sound theoretical understanding which she shares in a clear and accessible style.

In this second edition of her book she has updated and expanded the text in the light of recent research and extended her investigation of how young children learn in and through movement. There are now two chapters devoted to dance. The first of these suggests strategies for working with young children while the second suggests ways in which the expressive and artistic aspects of children's movement can be appropriately located within the 'Effective Framework for Adults Working with Children from Birth to Three', the 'Foundation Stage' and at Key Stages 1 and 2. Both these chapters, as all others throughout the book, highlight the interrelationship of theory and practice.

TINA BRUCE
Series Editor
September 2002

Acknowledgements

To all my colleagues, at various stages of my teaching career, I am grateful for the years of sharing which took place and for the wide range of opportunities given to me, many of which have provided material for my writing. And, of course, to the children whose movement continues to interest and delight me.

My involvement with two institutions has played an important part in all the teaching and research which I have undertaken. The first is the Laban Art of Movement Studio (now known as Laban) where my fascination with the field of human movement began. To Rudolf Laban, Lisa Ullman and my many teachers there I am grateful, and especially to Dr Marion North, OBE, who taught me so much about the theory and practice of movement observation and its importance in personality assessment. My experience at the Laban Studio was followed immediately with my time at the Froebel Institute College and here my appreciation is to Molly Brearley, CBE, Principal of the College at the time and to Chris Athey, MEd, author and formerly Principal Lecturer in Education and Leverhulme Research Fellow. Each in her own way has helped me towards an understanding of the rich variety of ways in which young children learn.

My thanks go to the parents, teachers and friends who allowed me to photograph their children and to record their activities and conversations. And to the parents who took photographs of their children for me. Their interest, curiosity and generosity have been an important source of encouragement. I hope that when they read what has been written and see the photographic images of their children they will understand what a significant contribution they have made. I am especially grateful to Terry Kane for his photographic contribution to the first edition and to the front cover of the second edition, to Niki Sianni for her photograph of 'Mothers and Toddlers' and to Catherine Ashmore for allowing the inclusion of her photographs of Hannah. I am indebted to Graeme Orrick, BSc, for the many hours he spent on the diagrams relating to Laban's work. The demands were considerable – his response always generous and informed. To Shu-Ying Liu I extend my appreciation for her permission to use an illustration of her research in Taiwan. I am particularly grateful to Dr Susan Danby for her detailed reading of the manuscript, for her constructive criticism and, above all, for sharing my interests. My sincere thanks go to Jean Jarrell MA for her ongoing support throughout the entire process, for allowing me to rehearse every idea that came to mind and entering into the debate.

Marianne Lagrange, Commissioning Editor, and Saleha Nessa, Assistant Editor and all the publishing team at Sage have given invaluable guidance throughout the writing process. I have greatly valued their involvement and interest.

Finally, I wish to convey appreciation to Professor Tina Bruce, my series editor, who has given me continuous support during the writing of this second edition. She has shared my interests and curiosity, and extended my thinking. I am most grateful to her for her encouragement, gentle guidance – and once again for keeping faith.

Preface for the 0–8 Series

The 0–8 Series has stood the test of time, maintaining a central place among early childhood texts. Practitioners have appreciated the books because, while very practical, the series presents a holistic approach to work with young children, which values close partnership with families and their communities. It is evidence based, drawing on theory and research in an accessible way.

The 0–8 Series, now being revised and updated, continues to deal with the themes of early childhood which have always been of concern and interest to parents, practitioners and the children themselves. The voice of the child has, since 1989, been under threat in education. Each author has made an important contribution in their field of expertise, using this within a sound background of child development and practical experience with children, families, communities, schools and other early childhood settings. The series consistently gives a central place to the interests and needs of children, emphasising the relationship between child development and the socio-cultural learning with which biological and brain development is inextricably linked. The voice of the child is once again being understood as being important if children are to develop and learn effectively, and if adults helping them to learn (teaching them) are to be effective in their work.

The basic processes of communication, movement, play, self-esteem and understanding of self and others, as well as the symbolic layerings in development (leading to dances, reading, writing, mathematical and musical notations, drawing, model-making) never cease to fascinate those who love and spend time with children. Some of the books in this series focus on these processes of development and learning, by looking at children and their contexts in a general way, giving examples as they go. Other books take a look at particular aspects of individual children and the community. Some emphasise the importance of rich physical and cultural provision and careful consideration of the environment indoors and outdoors and the way that adults work with children.

As Series Editor I am delighted to reintroduce the 0–8 Series to a new readership. The re-launched series enters a more favourable climate than the original series, which survived (and flourished) in a hostile climate of literacy hours for four-year-olds, adult-led learning, and a lack of valuing diversity, multi-lingualism, imagination and creativity. This revised and updated 0–8 Series will inform, support and inspire the next generation of early childhood practitioners in the important work they do, in a climate which will encourage rather than undermine.

I look forward to seeing the impact of the 0–8 Series on the next decade.

PROFESSOR TINA BRUCE
London Metropolitan University
October 2001

Introduction

In the seven years since this book was first published many changes have taken place. There have been significant publications in early childhood literature and a consequent increase in the understanding of young children and the variety of contexts in which they live and learn. The National Curriculum for pupils aged from five to eleven is fully operative and for the first time the Foundation Stage has been enshrined in law.

Personally, a second edition has meant a 'second chance'. A chance to re-visit concepts and children, to read extensively, to make new observations and attempt to translate generalities into specifics and problems into opportunities. I have also been able to extend the trans-global perspective by references to children beyond the UK – in Finland, France, Germany, Puerto Rica, and Taiwan.

Essentially, this book is about the multi-faceted role that movement plays in the lives of young children. It explores the nature and function of movement as a central part of their doing, thinking and feeling and highlights the pleasure and sense of well-being which is experienced as they are helped to come to maximise their bodily potential. It argues that attention given by adults to the development of their children's movement, and its significance in the learning process, is crucial right from the start of life. This is not only because it helps towards producing a well-tuned and articulate body, which in itself is a matter of considerable importance, but also because of the significant role movement plays in the development of feeling and thought.

At the hub of the book is a framework of movement which, presented in Chapter 1, permeates the text. Each of the chapters considers one particular set of ideas which gives it a specific emphasis. However, rather like movement itself, these ideas also find their place in other chapters. In this re-appraisal I have at times considered movement as a 'virtual' jigsaw puzzle where pieces fit, change and interlock, resulting in the uniqueness of each and every child.

Having observed ways in which they can be helped to develop thinking, expressing and socialising skills through movement, children are then seen in their roles as early performers, creators and spectators. The physical, intellectual and expressive implications of these roles are developed further in relation to dance in statutory education where ideas are suggested, debated and reflected upon at the Foundation Stage and at Key Stages 1 and 2.

Throughout, photographic illustrations inform the text. Because of the transient and momentary nature of human movement, at places they 'become' the text. The purpose of these, along with the classification, contextual examples, and general guidelines in which they are embedded, is to spark off procedures and practices – or ways and means – which seem most appropriate to a particular setting. Any specific use must be decided upon by the adults concerned, for not only are children unique but so also are the people who care for, nurture and educate them.

1

What is movement?

Everything that we discover about life, we discover through movement. Light waves reach the eye, sound waves contact the ear. Both smell and taste involve movement. Above all, our capacity to touch and move to gain further experience, confirms our awareness. (Hodgson 2001: 172)

This chapter provides a theoretical framework which serves as a reference point, or identity kit, for the many examples of children's activities which illustrate subsequent chapters of this book. It also provides a way of thinking about, supporting, enriching and recording children's movement for all those concerned with early childhood education.

The indivisibility of movement from human functioning may be one of the reasons why its importance in terms of child development is not always given the serious recognition it deserves. It is so inbuilt that it is not until movement is seen to be dysfunctional or ineffective in some way, such as in autism, depression, attention deficit hyperactive disorder, cerebral palsy or mood swings, that it emerges as a significant educational phenomenon. Postgraduate Dance Movement Therapy programmes on offer in the UK and elsewhere include diagnostic and treatment tools in their training and, increasingly, dance and movement join art, drama and music therapies in their bid to modify and enhance living. In the therapeutic context non-verbal communication of the body is 'incorporated with other research to refine coping distinctions and measure changes' and, as such, is universally acknowledged. (Bartenieff 1980: viii)

While welcoming such advancements in the therapeutic field, I believe that movement plays an equally important role in the growth, development and education of all children. However, because movement of young children is seen to be a part and parcel of their everyday lives the danger is that it can be taken for granted and overlooked in terms of its importance in the educational spectrum. Those concerned with child care and education may see no reason to classify and analyse something which seems so obvious. In contrast, however, as soon as children show the first signs of emergent reading skills, help is at hand; resources, methods and procedures are actively sought and discussion within and between family units abounds. Similarly, as children's interests in numeracy become apparent, parents are the first to join in the bigger/smaller, taller/shorter phase of discrimination. Even if parents and early childhood practitioners do not have detailed knowledge in these areas, realising its importance they seek it out and provide materials and experiences which assist learning at this stage.

In movement, too, important achievements are noted, valued and discussed with pride. Photograph albums and family CD libraries are filled with illustrations documenting such events as early, unsteady steps, digging in the sand, kicking a ball and swimming without support. But there the similarity ends. Although there is often movement-oriented provision in parks, playgrounds and gardens, detailed guidance for promoting, observing and recognising activities stimulating growth, development and creativity is far behind that in other areas of learning. Sometimes adults 'sense' what is needed to help children initiate, consolidate or progress in their movement activities but, however valuable and successful this sensing may sometimes seem to be, it needs to be related to a much larger canvas of knowledge. If parents and early years practitioners are to function knowingly it is necessary to extend beyond sensing. If they are to take responsibility for movement as an important area of children's experience then they need to know what 'constitutes' movement just as they need to know about all the other areas of learning for which they make provision.

The challenge was to find a model which was sufficiently proven and sufficiently flexible to relate to young children in a variety of situations: a model or framework which would establish general principles and cater not simply for provision but also for extended learning in objective and creative contexts. In choosing the framework used throughout this book acknowledgement is made to the theories of Rudolf Laban (1948, 1966, 1980) and those concerned with the development of his ideas including Bartenieff (1980), Lamb (1965), North (1972), Preston (1963), Preston-Dunlop (1998), Redfern (1973), Russell (1965) and Ullmann who continued his work after his death. After a remarkable life spent in researching movement in a variety of theoretical and practical contexts Laban's findings remain the most pertinent and relevant available today. As Hodgson (2001: 55) writes:

A good deal of Laban's work and theory forms the foundation of so much of our understanding of movement, that quite often people come to regard it now as common belief.

This allegiance may be partly due to his guiding principles which echo those of leading educational theorists of today, and which permeate my own thinking. Laban did not create a 'one and only' model but instead inspired others to take up and develop his principles in the variety of fields in which he worked. Preston-Dunlop (1998: cover), Laban scholar and researcher, writes:

His ideas have innovations not just in dance, but also in acting and performance, in the study of non verbal communication, in ergonomics, in educational theory and child development, in personality assessment and psychotherapy.

In her conclusion she comments (ibid.: 269):

Today his [Laban's] concepts are alive and well, adapted, pruned and developed to accommodate the needs and demands of the twenty-first century.

Theoretical framework of movement

Human movement is not only unique to the species but is also unique to each individual within it. To understand and recognise the complexity of individual uniqueness it is necessary first to establish the common denominators from which personal movement springs. **The body, the instrument of action**, is central to the classification of movement. Giving colour and form to the 'playing' of that instrument are three important and interrelated categories:

- *dynamics* which relates to how the instrument moves
- *space* which refers to ways in which the body inhabits and uses space
- *relationships* which identifies ways in which the body acts and interacts with people and objects.

THE INTEGRATION OF MOVEMENT

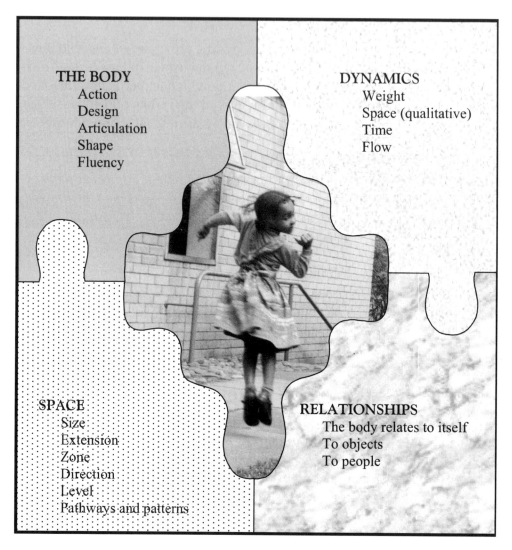

THE BODY
Action
Design
Articulation
Shape
Fluency

DYNAMICS
Weight
Space (qualitative)
Time
Flow

SPACE
Size
Extension
Zone
Direction
Level
Pathways and patterns

RELATIONSHIPS
The body relates to itself
To objects
To people

Figure 1 A general classification of movement in relation to young children from 0 to 8 years

The body: what takes place

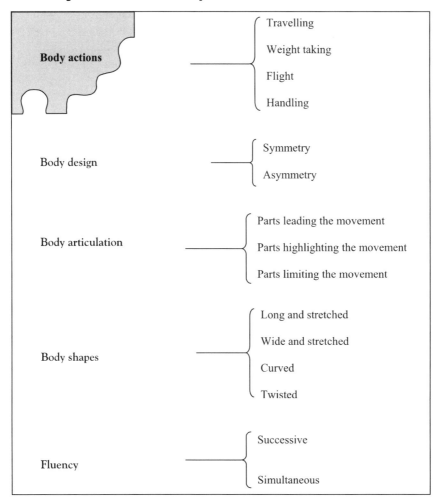

Figure 2   The body: the instrument of movement activity

The body in action

The body moving into action is a vital part of all movement activity whether it is spontaneous or in response to structured situations at home, in the play centre, in the supermarket, in the early years setting or at school. It is through the dynamic and spatial use of a growing number of separate and related actions, *action schemas*, that children become increasingly competent and versatile in a variety of movement situations.

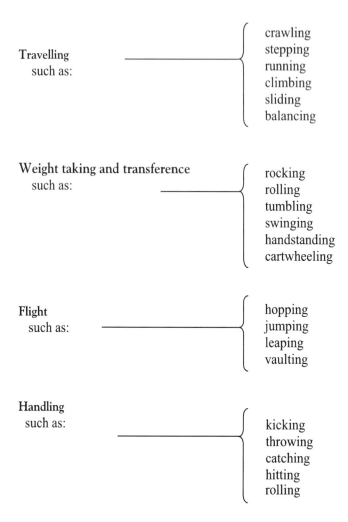

Travelling
such as:

- crawling
- stepping
- running
- climbing
- sliding
- balancing

Weight taking and transference
such as:

- rocking
- rolling
- tumbling
- swinging
- handstanding
- cartwheeling

Flight
such as:

- hopping
- jumping
- leaping
- vaulting

Handling
such as:

- kicking
- throwing
- catching
- hitting
- rolling

Figure 3   The body in action

At first actions of babies are restricted to the relatively confined spaces they inhabit and the people with whom they are in contact. Reaching, grasping, sucking, wriggling and kicking feature dominantly in the early months. As soon as they become more independently mobile they are able to invest their actions in spatial areas previously unavailable to them. The shuffling and crawling activities of babies develop into a range of *travelling* actions which typify the play of young children as they transport themselves from one place to another.

Sometimes children enjoy staying put in small pockets of space and explore actions which *support or transfer their weight*; they rock, roll over, turn upside down and, in all these activities, face different perspectives of their world. As they amass and develop a more complex range of action schemas so their perspective experience widens. The *Curriculum Guidance for the Foundation Stage* draws attention to the importance for children to see things from different perspectives such as from the top of a climbing frame, in a tunnel or below a box (QCA 2000: 102).

Actions associated with dexterity, involving *handling objects*, such as throwing, kicking and catching which feature in young children's 'games play', also have their early roots. The baby's grip and release of a rattle through to the sophisticated throwing and catching of the eight-year-olds represent another category of important body actions children gradually add to their repertoire.

Overcoming gravity and being in flight is a delight for all children and is something which remains with them throughout the first phase of living and beyond. Before they can manage to push off and make themselves airborne they jump from a stair, kerbstone or chair which, in reality, means *dropping* down rather than *jumping* down. Although at this stage they are not yet quite there, nevertheless the children are getting the feel of the activity. Being helped to jump by or with adults, willing to participate in the play situation, is a way of feeling what it is like – in this case *to be airborne* – an experience important to the development of any activity.

Parents and early childhood educators will immediately be able to think of some of the actions their children can perform, particularly those which are frequently repeated and that have become current favourites. They will also be able to recall ways in which some of these have developed over time. When, for example, a turn became a spin, when a jump came out of a run, and when a jump lasted long enough to make a shape or turn in the air such as the one shown in Photograph 1. Body action is an important ingredient of movement, particularly so for young children. Specific examples of body actions will be discussed in a variety of contexts in the chapters which follow.

Photograph 1   Turning in the air: two actions in one

Body design

Figure 4   The body is well designed

The general public, including children themselves, are increasingly design conscious. Designer labels on clothes, mobile phones and toys are firmly established as indicators of prestige. In the professional worlds of dance and sport, design characteristics of the human body are photographically captured in a range of athletic and artistic achievements, many of which seem to defy the expected range. So breathtaking are some of these achievements it is difficult to remember that they have their roots in the body of the newborn baby – that the nurturing of such potential lies in the hands of those who educate and care.

Through its natural structure and the number and arrangement of limbs, often the body of a baby is initially anatomically *symmetric* although very early on habitual ways of moving with emphasis on one side of the body over the other frequently involve the use of *asymmetry*. Apart from early reflex shaking and beating activities of very young babies, symmetry, brought about through equal emphasis of both sides of the body, is usually associated with evenness and involves movement characterised by control and balance. Examples of symmetry are swinging, exerting two-sided movement of arms and legs, a low squat position near the ground frequently adopted by young children, or engagement in a handspring enjoyed by eight-year-olds.

Asymmetric movement is recognised by the way one side of the body is emphasised more than the other and where there is a lack of equivalence between the two sides. In contrast to the even balance associated with symmetric movement, asymmetry is characterised by off-balance and less restrained movement which has a tendency to be 'ongoing'. Specific movement activities, such as early throwing behaviour, require an appropriateness of body design but, apart from these, both children and adults usually have a natural preference for either two-sidedness or one-sidedness. A quick glance at a group of children as they listen to a story, eat a meal or engage in dramatic play will give clear indications of their preferences.

Body articulation

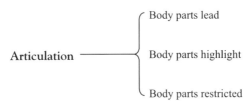

Articulation —

- Body parts lead
- Body parts highlight
- Body parts restricted

Figure 5 The body is well articulated

A well-articulated body can emphasise the use of one part or several parts of the body at will. These may lead the movement as the head does when 'being a plane' or where hands go first to meet the ground on the way to a handstand. Parts of the body may be given a role of importance and highlighted as in the way the hands wave or the feet tap dance. Highlighting the varied use of body parts is natural for children at early stages of learning and an important experience for both skilled and inventive performance. So, too, is the restricting of body parts, a limitation which children often impose upon themselves. 'No hands', a special favourite, is illustrated for us in Photograph 2 which shows Charlotte, aged seven, as she enjoys the see-saw.

Photograph 2   Self-imposed bodily restriction: no hands

Body shapes

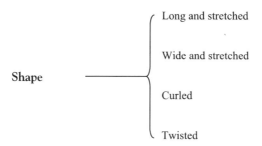

Shape ——————— Long and stretched

Wide and stretched

Curled

Twisted

Figure 6   The body can make a variety of shapes

Body shape refers to the form of the body when a position is held and there are four of these which can be easily identified in children's movement play.

Long and stretched

The first shape is *long and stretched* emphasising the use of one direction only. It stresses the dimension of length and body parts are aligned to produce the

Photograph 3   An elongated body shape

effect of elongation and narrowness. This shape is seen clearly as children tunnel their way through hollow tubes, play at parachuting, dive, attempt a netball or basketball shot, or are directed to stand up straight! In Photograph 3 Eleanor, aged two-and-a-half, is responding to a suggestion to stretch up as tall as she can. As she does so her body becomes narrow and long as she pierces the space in an upward direction.

The second body shape is also stretched but this time in *terms of width*. The natural tendency of two-dimensional movement results in this shape as arms and legs are stretched sideways into space, spreading away from the centre of the body and creating a tension between the limbs themselves. Children enjoy making two-dimensional star shapes early on, as shown by Lucy and her mother in Photograph 4. Sometimes this shape is used to suggest 'being big' or to provide a barrier to stop someone, or something, getting past.

Photograph 4   Wide and stretched: mother and daughter share a two-dimensional body shape

Jumping in a star shape soon becomes a favourite activity and is often seen as older children take off from walls, trees and apparatus or into the swimming pool. In swimming breaststroke the star shape, with its *two-dimensionality of movement*, is emphasised as a child's body travels through the water. The more complex activity of a cartwheel shows a moving, star-shaped image as the weight of the body is taken successively from hand to hand to foot to foot as the body revolves. It also serves a symbolic function in expressive movement. Spinning in a horizontal star shape may occur in a catherine wheel or spinning-top dance or performed simply for the circular movement sensation itself.

A third body shape, *three-dimensional in character*, which is essentially *rounded*, is often seen in rolling activities where the spine curves and the extremities meet – or almost meet – each other. The curve may sometimes be taken in the opposite direction, with the back of the head and the heels sharing the arc. This is a shape which, at later stages of growth and development, constitutes part of athletic or acrobatic activity as seen in a backward dive, a 'crab walk' or pole vault. In artistic terms, it is one often used by both contemporary and classical dancers.

The last of the four body shapes is *twisted* as different areas of the body pull against each other around one or more axes. It is much used by the seven- and eight-year-olds in dance and dramatic play associated with aspects of the natural environment such as gnarled trees, with wizards, sea monsters and other imaginary creatures. The sinuous way in which young bodies twist and turn in and out of railings, small spaces and almost impossible gaps also show this particular body shape to perfection.

Bodily fluency

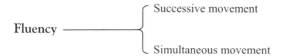

Figure 7   The body has a natural fluency

In *successive movement*, body parts are brought into play one after another in a wave-like, rippling action. Such movement has a fluidity about it and makes for continuity. It can be identified early on in the writhing of babies and, later, objectively in the movement of young children as they grasp a low-hanging branch and, starting with their feet, take their body through with the use of knees, hips, spine and head as they achieve balance the other side. *Simultaneous movement*, on the other hand, occurs when some and, at times all parts of the body move at the same time. The 'togetherness', implicit in simultaneous movement, is present throughout the whole action, from the moment it starts until the end of its passage. An obvious example of this is when babies bring all of themselves to their centre, perhaps in pain or delight, creating a small ball. At the other end of the age range we see young children of seven or eight years taking on the style of premier league players as they hurl their bodies across the space to 'save a goal'.

Dynamics: how movement takes place

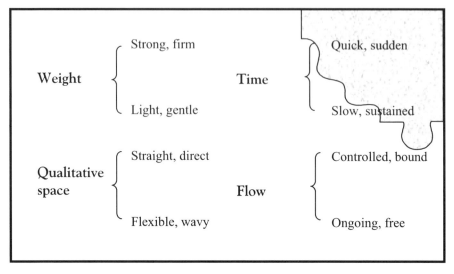

Figure 8   The body moves dynamically and rhythmically

All human activity is dynamically and rhythmically charged and structured. Young children, like people at every stage of life, are recognised by the dynamic and rhythmic make-up which personalises their style of moving. The combination and interrelatedness of the movement factors of weight, qualitative space, time and flow determine the rhythmic and dynamic differences between individual children and characterise 'how' they move. Sometimes specific actions require a particular rhythmic and dynamic mix if the response is to be effective; the *strong* leg action in kicking a ball, the *slow, careful* threading of shoe laces, the *vigorous* shaking of a rattle or tambourine. Making appropriate responses to specific daily challenges such as these implies a rich dynamic range from which to select: a range that needs stimulating, supporting and nurturing throughout the primary years.

Weight

Very young children, typically at about two years, understand the weight factor of movement mainly in terms of opposites, of movement being either *strong and forceful or light and gentle*. As their understanding increases, so finer discriminations of strength and force can be produced at will and in context.

Changes in the muscular tension of the body which result in changes of energy and force occur, for example, when children pit their energy against external structures. In order to pull up on the sides of a cot, onto a branch of a tree, or to climb a rope, a *strong grip* of the hands and *strength* in the shoulder girdle and arms are needed to lift the body in defiance of its own weight. Eight-year-old James, seen in Photograph 5 needed a tremendous amount of *strength and energy* to travel the full length of the overhead track. He helped himself by creating a swinging rhythm which took away some of the muscular strain as he transferred his weight from one ring to the next. *Strength and energy* are also required to jump far, high and wide, to kick a ball hard, and to effectively hammer a nail into a piece of wood. Movement can be more lightly and gently charged. A *delicate touch* is needed to make light brush marks on the paper, to stroke the hamster or to catch a soap bubble on an outstretched hand. In dance, *firmness* is brought into play where power and purpose are features of expression while *gentle, buoyant movement* is, as it were, finely tuned.

Photograph 5   Strength and energy are needed here

Qualitative space

Some movement can be described as very *straight, direct and thread-like* in appearance. Other movement has a *flexibility* which gives it a three-dimensional feel. This part of young children's dynamic movement make-up is perhaps less easy to observe in the early stages than the other three factors of weight, time and flow. Certain situations may require the use of one or the other of these space elements. For example, children may use *flexibility* in putting their arms into the sleeves of their coat, twisting in and out of the banisters or casting a magical spell. *Directness* features prominently where aiming is involved, in trajectory activities for instance or when a narrow focus is given to the task in hand as shown by Mark in Photograph 6 as he gives his entire attention to his modelling.

Photograph 6   Mark concentrates on his modelling

Time

Movement can be *speedy and sudden* as well as *slow and leisurely*, with degrees of differentiation between the two. *Fast and slow* are movements which appear early in the understanding of young children. Through experimenting they soon become aware that, for many of their activities, there is an appropriateness of speed: a *slow* stretching of the leg to find the section of the climbing frame or rung of the ladder which can safely take the weight of the body, a *quick* dash to get to the ball and the *lively quality* of the 'breeze' dance, are all examples of an appropriate use of time in the play of most four-, five- and six-year-olds. In addition to being *fast and urgent* and *slow and leisurely* there are many degrees along the continuum. As children gradually become more competent and use more and more of these segments of time, so ideas of *acceleration* and *deceleration* come into play, featuring prominently in the movement of children aged around six, seven and eight.

Flow

Flow refers to movement which ranges from being *restricted and bound* through to movement which is essentially *free and outgoing*. Descriptions of young children are often given by adults in terms of flow, with phrases such as 'outgoing', 'expansive', 'restrained' or 'withdrawn' giving clues to their behaviour. As well as being indicative of mood, the use of flow also features in the acquisition of skill, for example, in cutting paper, in making models, in learning to write or to play a musical instrument. At first, *bound flow*, associated with extreme care, reflects tentativeness. But, as skill improves, so does the sense of confidence expressed by the freeing of flow. As Roberts (2002: 105) suggests, having a sense of mastery is deeply linked with feelings of self-esteem. Activities carried out on agility apparatus involve a *range of flow responses*, freer flow giving continuity to the activity and restraint, involving the ability to stop and hold back, helping to prevent accidents to the mover and other children in the vicinity.

Dynamics in context

Dynamic and rhythmic components of movement have no particular value in themselves. What is important is that they are used appropriately. It is 'no better' to be able to move with sudden, quick vitality than with sustainment and leisure. Strong action is 'no better' than a gentle, fine touch. Assessment depends entirely upon the context in which movement occurs and, therefore, it is important to have as wide a range of dynamics as possible in order to make appropriate selections and combinations. Readers will notice the absence of the diagrammatic breakdown of the dynamics section of the movement framework. In order to avoid repetition this appears in Chapter 6 where children's expressive behaviour is considered in more depth.

Space: the medium in which movement takes place

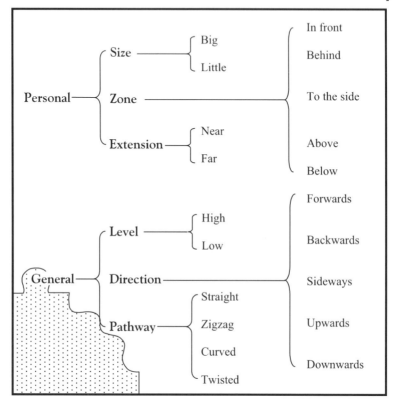

Figure 9   Space: the medium in which movement takes place

Space is referred to here in two ways; first as the *personal space surrounding the child's body*, sometimes referred to as the kinesphere (Laban 1948) and, sec-ondly, *as the general space which is beyond personal space and bounded by the par-ticular confines within which any of the children's activity takes place*. Personal space is as far as children can reach round about themselves when they are situated in one place. Their general space might be the playpen, the sofa, the stairs, the climbing frame in the garden, swings and roundabouts in the park, the adventure playground, a specially designated section of the nursery or the hall of the infant school. Children carry their personal space with them as they travel in the general space in which they move.

Size and extension

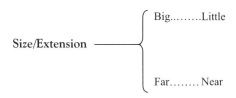

Figure 10   Big and little – near and far

In the movement world of young children, size is usually associated with extension and so these two elements of personal space are considered together. In identifying movements which are kept near the body or extend a long way from it, and are large or small, it is easy to conjure up images of children who use such notions frequently. 'Near', 'far', 'big' and 'little' feature prominently in the learning of young children and their experience in this area is vitally important.

Zone

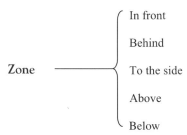

Figure 11   In front, behind, to the side, above and below

The structure of the body gives rise to spatial areas of movement with different parts of the body having their 'natural' zones. Young children use their arms a great deal to gesture in the upper areas of space in front of, behind, to the side and above their bodies. This natural zoning occurs similarly with the legs which step, gesture and jump in the lower regions of personal space. Fun and excitement may be brought about by varying the natural use of zones; moving around with hands grasping ankles and hanging upside down on a ladder are just two such examples of inverted zoning which children seek naturally for themselves or are encouraged to try out by others.

Direction

Figure 12   Forwards, backwards, sideways, upwards and downwards

Direction is a development of zoning. The three bodily dimensions of *length, breadth and depth* provide the basis of all orientation in space; the length of the body gives rise to the directions of up and down, the width of the body to left and right, and the depth of the body to forwards and backwards. It is obvious from the skeletal structure of the body that forwards is the most natural direction in which to move. When babies are able to stand unaided this is usually the first direction taken when they begin to walk. It is not, however, only the dimensions of the body but also awareness of different body parts which help the understanding of direction. Apart from crawling, when the head leads the baby forwards while parallel to the ground, the head is naturally associated with movement of an upward direction while the feet give a sense of going down. The sides of the body, together with the arms, familiarise children with sideways, while the chest and back of their bodies are strongly associated with forwards and backwards respectively.

In encouraging 'dance-like' play, young children are best helped to appreciate directions by references to the body with suggestions to 'follow their noses', or their 'heels go first'. At about six years of age, when directional awareness is less dependent on reference to their own bodies, children can cope with general suggestions to move in different directions. It is useful to remember that while in 'dance-like' activity directions can be used freely and creatively, in games-oriented activity direction is employed according to the demands of a particular game and, therefore, opportunities for variation are limited. Nevertheless, direction is an important factor in games and games-like activities, first, in action skills such as kicking, hitting and throwing and, later, for the seven- and eight-year-olds, in tactical play.

Level

Figure 13 High and low

Level, or the height at which any action takes place, ranges from *low to high* with many variations between the two extremes. Again levels are personal, in that they are related to the body.

- Low level is deep and around the floor.
- Medium level is situated approximately at mid-body.
- High level is above the head.

Young children often use these ideas in their play. One well-known example is in 'family play' where one child bends the knees and shuffles along at low level, being the baby, while the other walks on toes, or puts on high-heeled shoes, in order to 'become' the grown-up and use authority from 'on high'. Characteristically, young children enjoy extremes as they move freely or respond to suggestions from adults or friends. They know and delight in the use of high and low as they move. The 'in between' medium level is used less frequently and with less understanding by the very young. It is more likely to be passed through en route than actively engaged in its own right. Later, in relation to the young child's increasing ability to recognise smaller divisions and to order them sequentially, usually around six or seven years, it assumes greater importance.

Pathways and patterns

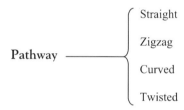

Figure 14 Straight, zigzag, curved and twisted

Pathways are important in children's spontaneous play. Two-, three- and four-year-olds mainly travel in straight lines and curves while by about six or seven, children may be expected to respond to challenges to move in all four of the following ways: *straight, angular, curved and twisted*. Challenging children to move in particular pathways implies considerable knowledge on their part and understanding in this sphere of movement comes about slowly.

The challenge to 'make a straight movement in space' implies:

- no change of direction
- an uninterrupted pathway
- a single focus.

The challenge to 'make an angular movement in space' implies:

- movement that changes direction acutely
- an awareness of sharp angles
- a zigzag movement.

The challenge to 'make a curved movement in space' implies:

- a directional change that is gradual
- an awareness of smooth, even movement
- no hint of angularity.

The challenge to 'make a twisted movement in space' implies:

- movement which curves first in one direction and then in another
- an awareness that movement is going back on itself creating a pattern similar to an S or figure of eight.

Movement patterns, such as those seen in track marks left in a wet sand tray, in a painting or when walking down a muddy lane, are situations where the movement is two-dimensional in nature. When, however, children move in what might be called 'air space', movement becomes more flexible and three-dimensional. As well as those across the floor, pathways and patterns in the air created by gestures of the arms are an important element of dance. In most agility-type activity, floor patterns assume greater significance than air patterns and in many games ground pathways are major considerations, often coming about by chance according to how the game develops and the kinds of tactics involved.

Relationships: the moving body interrelates

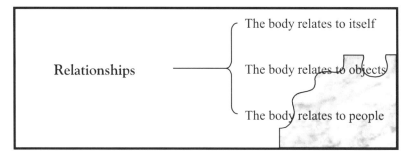

Figure 15   The body relates to itself, to objects and to people

The body relates to itself

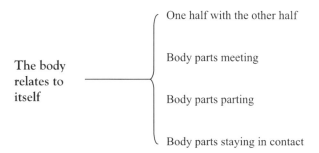

Figure 16   The body relates to itself

One of the growing excitements for young children comes about through a gradual realisation of the various ways in which different parts of the body relate to one another. Sometimes the relationship occurs between large sections of the body. As seen in Photograph 7, Hannah, aged four, maintains a strong, wall-like lower half while her top half bends over to look through her legs. Other examples include making a back for someone to jump over or providing a gap through which to pull a friend. These are relationships between parts of the body which children knowingly create for themselves.

Photograph 7   Looking through legs gives a different perspective

As a child's awareness of individual body parts increases, so, too, does the sophistication with which these parts relate to each other. In 'dance play', for example, not only may the palms of the hands touch each other as in clapping but sides, backs and fingertips may make contact in a variety of ways. The right hand wrapping round the body to arrive near to, or on, the left shoulder brings about a different expression from the right elbow resting on the right hip. In handling apparatus the body tends to play a participatory and supporting role while specific parts are engaged in action, for example, when an arm and hand are involved in bouncing a ball.

Relationships between body parts also involve dynamic, rhythmic and spatial nuances. *Cartwheels* and *handstands* demand refined articulation of the 'relevant' parts of the body and careful spacing between them as the weight is adjusted throughout the activity. Weight adjustment is also important in all sorts of *climbing activities* where hands and feet work in synchronisation as children travel along, upwards or downwards. Climbing is an extremely complex business and early attempts are often restrained and slow. It is as though the children are pausing for thought or collecting themselves, which is, in a sense, what they are doing. As if to help the children on their way adults are sometimes tempted to give physical assistance, even to the extent of lifting the foot of a young child and placing it on the next rung. This might seem helpful but as the foot is momentarily taken out of the child's control the important changes of body weight which give significant signals to the child are temporarily removed. Although the pattern of hand–foot co-ordination is differently sequenced as children become more skilled, the weight adjustment remains central to the activity of climbing itself.

In Photograph 8, Josh, two-and-a-half years old, shows confidence which

Photograph 8   Hands and feet move simultaneously as distance is estimated

Photograph 9   Josh takes a well earned and needed rest

can be seen in the lovely, long stretch of his body and the careful placing of hands and feet as he estimates the distance between the rungs. Although, on this occasion, he missed a rung at one point on the way up, he resumed climbing almost immediately, his hands and feet easily regaining their former co-ordinated pattern. The quiet assurance with which he recovered and took up where he left off is due, in part, to the support of his mother and, in part, to the fact that he had experienced this activity before. It was interesting to observe that Josh took the opportunity to rest on a conveniently placed flat surface of the climbing frame and to be still after he completed his climb. Action and recovery are natural partners in early childhood activity and children may often be seen in attitudes of repose on agility apparatus. This is absolutely normal, a time to be respected and not to be rushed.

The body relates to objects

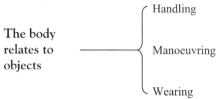

Figure 17   The body relates to objects

Activity related to objects which can be moved and manipulated causes the body to behave in different ways from movement related to the stable environment. Children's play with hoops, bats and balls, where there is considerable unpredictability and where chance frequently dictates the next move, is different in kind. In bouncing a ball against the floor or a wall, effective contact has to be made between the hand and the ball. This is difficult for very young children and few under five can manage to keep such an activity going for long. Even greater demands are made when the same activity is carried out with a bat instead of the hand. Now an additional relationship has to be made between the child and the bat in an attempt to make contact with the ball. Contact between objects, in this case a bat and a ball, is brought about by the use of the body in time and space.

In dance, activity related to objects happens less frequently although early dance experiences often include successful handling of balloons, ribbons and drapes. However, while drapes and dressing-up clothes may facilitate expressive movement, early childhood practitioners will recognise how very young children, who usually move with ease and fluency, can suddenly become wooden and stick-like when encouraged to move with a tambourine, hand castanet or set of bells. But by the age of seven and eight children can cope with and enjoy dancing with percussion. Instead of the restriction found in the movement of younger children, they manage to make the musical instrument an extension of their body as they move. Some also cope well with the increased complexity of dancing with two instruments, such as a drum and beater, demanding grip from both hands – a feat outside the realm of the youngest children. However, all children enjoy moving with materials and other objects and, as long as their use is self selective or introduced in an informed and sensitive way, they delight in dancing in this way.

The body relates to other people

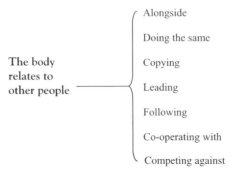

Alongside

Doing the same

The body
relates to
other people

Copying

Leading

Following

Co-operating with

Competing against

Figure 18   The body relates to other people

Photograph 10   Callum watches his mother to 'time' his jump

Associating with other people is an integral part of the movement activities of young children. They work alongside others sharing space and equipment in the sense that they allow it to happen and, sometimes, when one child initiates an activity two or three others will join in. 'Follow my leader' is a popular movement theme that involves an early, uncomplicated relationship. At its most basic the followers conform only to the leader's track – *where* it is taking place. This gradually develops so that more and more of the detail of the movement content – *what* the leader is doing – is taken on by the follower. By the time children reach seven or eight, identical complex 'I move as you move' sequences are often in evidence. This activity demands clarity and consistency from the leader and detailed observation and selection of appropriate movement patterns on the part of the follower.

Children include adults and their peers in negotiating relationships; they climb, pass and travel round, up and over them. Co-operating alongside, and competing with, characterise two more of the social relationships which young children experience. During an activity time together Callum and his mother have danced, jumped and played football. Photograph 10 shows Callum looking at his mother's feet, 'checking' when she is about to jump so that he can match his jump to hers and take off at the same time.

Summary

The main concern of this chapter has been to establish, comment upon and illustrate the four separate categories of human movement in the ways in which they relate to young children. These categories are closely and intricately related. The following chapters will look in greater detail at integrated patterns of children's activity as they learn to move more effectively and expressively, and move to learn in terms of thinking and socialising.

2

Learning to move

The early years are exciting times for children's development as they grow, changing in shape and size, and for children's movement development as they gain in body awareness and as they explore the vast range of available movement experiences within their environment.   (Maude 1996: 187)

The main purpose of this chapter is to highlight ways in which movement relates to and is part of the physical development of young children who, from the moment they are born, learn to move in increasingly skilful and versatile ways. It is impossible to isolate this one area of learning and important to stress that what follows is written in the knowledge that movement is part of the larger canvas of young children's development. For example, learning to move cannot be divorced from the fact that physically oriented experiences, as well as cultural and social experiences, encourage the ways and extent to which the brain develops. In making a case for an educational system that matches different kinds of learning tasks Colin Blakemore (1998) suggests that different learning modes are linked with the brain's passage through spans of specific sensitivity.

Calvin draws attention to the need for children to improvise and involve themselves with new learning experiences. He associates play and versatility in the brain and points out that:

We need an early childhood curriculum which helps children try out how to do things they don't know how to do – yet – in ways which are biologically appropriate.   (Calvin 1997: 26)

From the first moments after birth babies make their needs and feelings known through movement and gather to themselves a whole variety of impressions which help to create an ever-changing picture of their personal world. Right from the start, the environment and the supporting, sharing, facilitating roles of family, friends and practitioners are immensely important for the development of the newborn infant. All developmental sequences have their own emphasis in the overall developmental process but it is essential to get off to a good start in providing significant personal and environmental contexts. Research published by the Carnegie Corporation (1994: 12) 'highlights the importance of the first two years of life when the development of connections between brain cells depends on whether children receive appropriate stimulation'.

The biological processes of growth and maturation, established in the womb, are seen soon after birth and remain of central interest to family and friends throughout childhood and adolescence. Physical and movement development takes place from the head downwards and from the centre of the body outwards in what Maude (1996: 188–9) calls cephalo-caudal and proximo-distal development. Very early motor responses are common to most babies and the order in which they appear is mainly predictable. For example, co-ordination of large body movements precedes precise and specific movements, and unilateral movement follows the bi-lateral movement that characterises activity in the early months. However, it is important to remember that the rate of development is very much an individual affair and to a considerable extent is associated with appropriate environmental provision within a wide range of hereditary, environmental, cultural and social settings.

Knowledge in the making

Although the movement of babies may appear to be relatively gross and unfocused, almost at once they show clear signs of responding to the peopled world around them. Schaffer (1996) puts forward the view that babies are born attuned to visual and auditory stimuli provided by other people. Dependent upon the social and cultural setting, most babies can usually recognise and respond to one or two particular relationships through sound, sight and touch within a matter of weeks. As they come to recognise the faces of other people they regularly meet so they enlarge their circle of familiar and friendly contacts. Referring to the work of Schaffer, Karstadt and Medd (2000: 35) are in agreement that 'over time babies become involved in a multi-person world, with many interactions and relationships occurring beyond this initial pairing'. It is not, however, just the face, per se, that is recognised but also the expression that the face takes on at different times.

Carter (1998: 85) makes the point that 'Children respond appropriately to facial expressions almost from the time they are born, but they get better at it as they get older' and goes on to associate the improvement with the maturation of the frontal lobes of the brain, the area concerned with emotion. Roberts and Tamburrini (1981: 47) comment that it is usually at about seven months, when faces are appreciated in greater detail, that initial anxiety is expressed when confronted with strange and unfamiliar faces. However, it is worth considering that the anxiety may relate not just to the unfamiliar structure but also to a facial expression that is not among the ones the infant knows. There is a parallel to be drawn here with the recognition of individual voices as perceived through the tone, volume and rhythmicality of the spoken word. Such observations help to explain why familiar visual or sound patterns 'delivered' by a stranger may bring forth 'dis-ease' or even distress, instead of intended comfort or delight.

Photograph 11   Zach has just learned to roll over

As well as responding to other people, babies respond to their own personal needs. They make progressively successful attempts to locate the source of food, to suck, to grasp or to alter the position of the body. Through such body movements Gerhardt (1973: 1) suggests the young child discovers consistencies which, in turn, create patterns of response. She calls these 'knowledge in the making'. In Photograph 11 Zach, aged twenty-five weeks, is learning to roll over and reach out to his toys.

The ways in which young children manage the length, height, weight and proportions of their bodies as they grow and develop can seem little short of a miracle, particularly as the relationship of the dimensions and proportions of the body changes so much through the years. Jackson (1993: 28) comments:

> *The vitality and speed of change is astonishing. Growing up is like a complex, fast moving game, where not only the rules and goal posts keep changing but also the players themselves.*

It is vitally important that all those who share in child care and education, are aware of the physical changes through which their children are progressing. Only then can they maintain an active part in identifying, extending and enriching the many experiences which make for flexible and mobile development. Continuing appropriate involvement of this sort provides important contributions to the physical, social and cognitive make-up of a young child.

Early 'handling' experiences

The first two years of early childhood feature a high level of 'handling' on the part of parents and early childhood practitioners, usually the highest level throughout childhood. In such handling situations the 'state' of infants may range from quiet, peaceful sleep to agitated, wakeful activity. Those new to caring for young infants will recognise the varied demands in trying at one moment to keep hold of a slippery, wriggling baby and, at another, to handle an intense, non-giving 'ramrod'. Many of the appropriate handling responses are learnt 'on the job' and parents and carers involved in constant daily care soon find a familiarity born of practice, knowing 'what' to do and 'how' to do it.

During the early months, parents interact with their babies using a personal range of sophisticated movement 'ingredients' as if to pass on something of their chosen patterns, actions and moods – which is just what they do. At this stage there is a large contrast between the variety, skill and refinement of movement with which adults function and the early, unsophisticated movements of the young children they live with and care for. The period of 'handling play' is an important part of the development of babies and gives an early start in the appreciation of a rich 'vocabulary of movement'. Being picked up, held upright, put down, turned over and made comfortable, are just a few of the many handling activities that take place daily and which babies recognise and play their part in. Sometimes, specific parts of the handler's body take on importance and have special meaning; the hands that stretch out, the arms that hold and the lips that kiss. Even very young babies contribute to these handling activities, for example, they 'activate' their bodies as arms extend to pick them up or purse their lips to share a kiss. On other occasions, instead of parts of the handler's body being all important, it is the expressive quality of a specific action which makes an impression. For example, young infants can feel and respond to differences between the strength and firmness of a lift, the gentleness of a caress and the vitality of a succession of lively, facial gestures especially designed to make them laugh.

In responding knowingly to an increasing number of people they see around them young infants can recognise people by hearing them as well as by seeing them move. The light, crisp steps of one, the heavy, regular tread of another and the rapid patter of a third come across as distinct dynamic patterns associated with particular individuals who currently inhabit their world. '*I can hear you*' as well as '*I can see you*' are early play observations of young children and feature dominantly in the lives of those who have restricted or no visual sight.

Expressive interaction

By the time they are involved in the education and caring of young children, adults have developed a vast range of movement 'ingredients' which they can mix and match to suit particular occasions. It is from this extensive movement repertoire that they select appropriate expression of voice and bodily gesture when interacting with young children. In responding to a young infant who is fractious and ill at ease a quiet, soothing tone, accompanied by a rocking or stroking action involving the movement elements of sustainment and gentleness, often has a positive effect. The success of this expressive interaction is seen, first, in the way the infant shares the newly created mood of calm with the handler and, secondly, how the mood change continues over time. In a similar way, a short, brisk and lively movement and tone of voice used in a time of shared play produces a different mood in the young infant and is invigorating rather than soothing in effect.

Photographs 12 and 13 show a situation of mood-sharing and modification. Bethany, aged twenty months, managed to turn the key on the inside of the bedroom door locking herself in while her mother was next door in the bathroom. She was heard crying and was clearly distressed. Her mother, Lindsey, could talk to her through the door but was unable to make physical contact. Eventually, a neighbour fetched a ladder, climbed through the window and opened the door. Mother and daughter were reunited. Photograph 12 was taken immediately following the 'adventure' and shows Lindsey comforting a distressed Bethany. Their arms are entwined and bodily contact is close. They almost merge. Photograph 13, taken a few minutes later, shows

Photograph 12 Lindsey holds Bethany close to her

Photograph 13 Lindsey helps Bethany to regain her confidence

Bethany, now soothed by her mother's sideways rocking action and calm, peaceful conversation. As she recovered, Bethany released her tight hold and assumed a vertical position. She partially turned towards her mother who, while maintaining a close 'face-to-face' contact, encouraged space to develop between them. Bethany's confidence is clearly returning.

To move appropriately is a sign of development

Acting appropriately means being able to respond to perceived needs in the most suitable manner. This is particularly relevant in the case of movement. While young sisters and brothers regularly see the ways in which adults success- fully handle a newcomer in the family unit, it is interesting to observe that an appropriate selection of movement ingredients is not always readily available to them. This is because they are still developing their own personal framework of movement and can sometimes only manage to 'approximate' to what is needed in specific situations and at particular times. Consequently, the well- intentioned kiss can be rough, the cuddle too tight and the rocking of the push-chair too vigorous. Young siblings need encouragement to acquire the app- ropriate 'movement mix', an encouragement that has to extend beyond on-the- spot verbal advice of adults 'not to be too rough', 'not to hold too tight' or 'to slow down'. They need help to recognise what is needed in a particular situation, to develop their personal movement repertoire and make relevant selections. As well as participating in a wide range of movement experiences to increase their own repertoire it is important to find situations which encourage the use of particular movement attributes – situations where they can try them out. The use of a range of gentle dynamics in stroking a rabbit, treading heavily in order to leave footprints in the sand, and squeezing paint from a resistant tube are important activities in establishing a wide menu of movement upon which to draw. Wheeling trolleys, building towers, setting out cups and saucers, dressing, undressing, rocking dolls and 'being the baby' all play an important role in understanding what is needed to act and interact appropriately.

Early rhythmic play: accents and emphasis

It is interesting to watch how adults playing with their babies use varying emphases or accents in their movement. One example of a well-known 'game' is where an adult or sibling makes a movement starting some way away from the baby which, as it gets nearer, gathers speed and force and culminates in a moment of excitement as the baby is picked up. Often some sound or nonsense 'word play' accompanies the game and is an integral part of it. Starting from nothing and gradually gathering force and energy in this way is an example of *impactive* movement and sound. When this rhythmic play becomes well established the baby begins to anticipate the process and share its distinctive patterning.

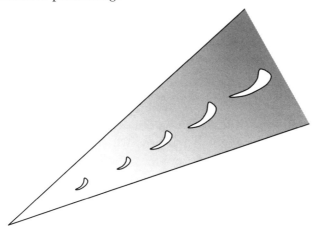

Figure 19   Impactive movement with stress at the end of the phrase (Davies, 1994)

Another well-known rhythmical game begins the other way round with the baby being lifted into the air with a strong, emphatic flourish which gradually fades away to nothing as he or she is lowered with decreasing speed and force. This movement pattern which explodes and gradually diminishes, again often accompanied by sound, is an example of *impulsive* movement.

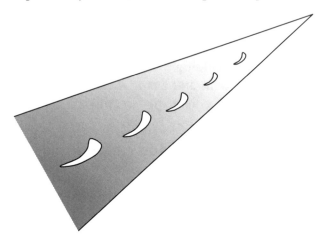

Figure 20 Impulsive movement with stress at the start of the phrase (Davies, 1994)

Allen, Lilley and Smith (2000: 165) highlight the importance of such increasing and decreasing sound patterns as assisting in the formation of the experiential basis for the continuously expanding world of the child:

> *Awareness of fixed sound sources, sounds getting closer and sounds moving further away, gradually combine with visual perception and recognition to provide infants with additional clues as to what is happening in their world.*

Apart from these intentionally designed play activities, it is useful for parents and 'handlers' to check occasionally that the general movement phrases they use when interacting with their young children are sufficiently varied. Most adults have preferred movement patterns which they use to communicate and by which they become well known. In terms of speaking, too, parents may recognise themselves as either preferring sentence construction which is *impulsively* structured with the momentum at the start of the sentence, or being *impactive* in their articulation making the end of the sentence a punch-line. Such individually pronounced, and often repetitive, associated move-ment and speech patterns are the stuff of impersonations both in terms of professional entertainment and at the more amateur level of family 'take-offs'. Although an occasion of fun, such occasions alert us to just how pronounced and habitual our movement and speech make-up really is. They also show how our movement and speech patterns are picked up by our children. As North writes (1972: 6):

> *Young children respond spontaneously to the movement of another person –*
> *'see' or 'feel' or 'experience' the person as a whole, through their whole being*
> *with a kinaesthetic sense, without analysing or verbalizing.*

Developing shared play

A variety of movement play with accents placed at different places along the stream of activity, gives the young infant an early experience of 'shared' rhythmical phrasing. Photograph 14 shows Sanna, from Finland, and her baby of three months enjoying a period of rhythmic play together. Sanna employs a rich range of bodily and qualitative movement when she plays with Aarne. Until now she has been mainly lifting and lowering him on her lower leg, an activity he has come to know and to enjoy. This is the first time their rhythmic play has taken on this particular pattern and, in contrast to his previous familiar activity, Aarne is clearly not yet at ease. But as the new game is repeated and he extends his range of individual and shared schemas

Photograph 14
Early rhythmic play

he will soon experience renewed confidence and enjoyment.

Rhythmic play of this kind continues to be important throughout the early years. Archie, aged eighteen months, is seen in Photographs 15–18 responding to the different 'movement conversations' with his parents. Having come to know and trust individual encounters with his father and mother Archie confidently enjoys being passed and then gently thrown between them. His delight is clear as he participates in their individual and joint rhythms and expresses his own.

Photograph 15
Archie and his mother play together

Photograph 16
Archie and his
father play together

Photograph 17   Sharing rhythms while 'passing between'

Photograph 18   Archie 'flying between'

Alexandra, who is three, also enjoys periods of rhythmic play. Her antici-
pation and contribution to these take on a more complex form than Archie's.
In order to jump into her father's arms she makes a circuit of climbing and
travelling on the agility frame to arrive at the steps from which she takes off
each time. First, she steadies herself on the steps and then, as if to jump, she
puts out her arms and leans forward towards her father who puts his arms

Photograph 19   Learning to launch

around her waist and lifts her high into the air. She has not yet acquired the understanding or the physical power of propulsion necessary to jump from the steps, although all the emergent signs are there. With lots of jumping experience to come, watching her six-year-old brother jump from the top step high into the air before being caught, and with the continuing support of her father, she will soon be able to launch herself into his arms.

Ongoing movement development

A whole range of sensory-motor actions arise from the basic, reflex actions of sucking, swallowing and grasping of pre-natal and post-birth activity. These follow each other in rapid succession during the first two years, being mainly concerned with postural control, manipulation, balance and locomotion. As babies grow and develop they delight those around them by adding new actions which they constantly repeat, vary and combine in different ways. These 'schemas' of action are described by Athey (1990: 36) as 'patterns of repeatable actions that lead to early categories and then to logical classifications'. Two further definitions of schemas which are helpful here are given by Neisser (1976: 111) who describes them as 'dynamic, active, information-seeking structures', and by Schmidt who, according to Magill (1998: 43), uses his schema concept to describe two control components involved in the learning and control of skills.

Actions carried out by babies and very young children are many and varied, curtailed principally by the relatively confined areas in which they take place; the carrycot, the high chair, on the rug or in the bath. At this active, but zone-restricted, stage family and friends frequently offer first-time parents such advice as 'wait until he is moving around' or 'you soon won't be able to leave her alone for a minute'. What these friends are predicting is the number of new and more complex actions young children add to their collections as soon as they can reach many more things in an increasingly accessible environment. It is at this stage that the needs for safety and opportunity coincide. While ensuring a stimulating and opportunity-filled environment we need to be careful not to leave potentially harmful materials and obstacles in the way of young children.

In terms of development young children both increase the number of actions they can do and develop and refine the skill with which those actions are carried out. This is an achievement which takes time and practice. Improved skill acquisition comes about partly through repetition in a familiar situation, for example climbing stairs or steps over and over again. It also occurs as a result of adapting a particular action by trying the action schema out in different settings; climbing garden walls, trees, ladders and ropes. In the first of these skill-oriented activities, the repetition of a discrete activity has as its main intent a specific, co-ordinated movement pattern. Magill (1998) advises that in a successive stage the performer (*in this context the child*) learns to achieve optimal performance of the skill in various situations.

Although movement development is still generally linear and predictable, as shown in the way children acquire motor skills, it would be a mistake to think that maturation alone is totally responsible for such development. It is a case of 'use it or lose it' and exposure to a wide selection of environmental opportunities plays an important part in the developmental process. A rich and varied environment is not a luxury but a necessity during the early years of life. In highlighting the interwoven elements of maturation and experience, and the key role they play in the development process, Gallahue (1989: 15) refers to the concept of *adaptation* to explain the complex interplay between forces within the individual and the environment.

It may be helpful to look in greater detail at the development of particular actions that characterise early childhood. There are many interesting and important actions that could be used as illustrations here and it has been difficult to make a choice. The following, both of which were introduced briefly in Chapter 1, have been selected for further consideration because they are constantly in use in three different settings – at home, in leisure settings and in professional contexts – and are carried on throughout life. They are:

- *balancing*, from the range of locomotor abilities
- *throwing*, from the manipulative range of abilities.

Balance

Balance is a complex activity, a core element of movement activity drawing upon visual, tactile and vestibular factors. It plays a significant role in the early years for, as stressed by Magill (1998: 280), 'It is a fundamental ability to many different skills'. As children travel through the various stages of balance control, the provision of stimulating environmental challenges and interaction with parents, teachers and friends, is all-important. It is through such provision and accompanying conversation that a well-educated and finely tuned body emerges. On the other hand, lack of appropriate provision can result, at best, in less than articulate movers and, at worst, in children who are physically inept, lack bodily confidence and, as a sad consequence, are in danger of being overlooked or even bullied.

Standing

Although the many and varied ways in which babies engage in early forms of movement across the floor are of great interest, the attention and degree of delight given to the first attempts of a young child to stand unaided are perhaps without match. At first the arms and hands are held away from the body and used in a mobile way, almost as regulatory wings. And, initially, for a short period, eyes are often cast down as if to make sure the ground stays where it is. But once their balance is mastered young children are able to view the world from a more or less vertical stance. This means getting used to things and people being differently positioned. Undoubtedly it feels quite different for young children to be this way up for long periods of time. In the words of Gerhardt (1973: 21), they 'align the world in relation to this new verticality'. Melville-Thomas (1993: 7), a dance movement therapist who has worked with children with a range of emotional and learning difficulties puts it this way:

> *One of the major changes in movement development is the achievement of verticality – being able to stand up by oneself. This is a good example of how a change in co-ordination leads to different perceptions and new possibilities for the child – the effect of standing up, and how the child feels about himself, and relates to others when he can stand – the meaning of standing up.*

The furniture walkabout

As proficiency in standing develops, the 'furniture walkabout' becomes a much practised and familiar activity. When familiarity is established to such a degree that the walkabout is carried out with confidence, and with few if any misjudgments, it is important to make changes in the position and relationship of furniture. These changes, calling for a different perception and movement response, should be fairly large and obvious at first. Perhaps just 'swapping' the positions of a stool and armchair. Making even such minimal changes implies that parents and carers realise that a child has reached what

Vygotsky (1978: 86) calls the *zone of actual development* and know that it is time to progress to the next stage of proximal or *potential development.*

This important developmental phase is a time when children may need a bit of help. Perhaps in asking them to point to the different placing of the furniture in the room – an observation quiz – or letting them watch, even participate in, the armchair and stool changeover. Dynamic equilibrium is dependent upon a sensing of body awareness that becomes increasingly detailed as finer adjustments of balance are called for so, where the rearrangement incorporates a more difficult climbing feat, an adult or 'senior peer' may need to be ready to give a helping hand. Later on, smaller and less obvious furniture moves can be incorporated until young children can cope with all the challenges presented and are able, quite literally, to 'take everything in their stride'.

The day in which young children make the transition, if only momentarily, from dependence on people or furniture to taking first steps without support is, as Roberts and Tamburrini (1981: 78) suggest, hailed as a red letter day in the family circle. But, as previously suggested, a great deal of practice is needed, in terms of balance, co-ordination and control of speed and direction, for further development of this newly emerging skill. To manage to do something once or twice is no guarantee of permanent skill acquisition. As Bruce (1987: 49), writing with reference to Bruner's notion of 'scaffolding', suggests, 'because a child cannot perform, or can only perform falteringly, does not mean that he/she is not ready for the task'.

Walking

As progress in early locomotion is made, the balancing role of the arms is gradually reduced and eventually disappears. Meanwhile tottering and walking, involving feedback from skeletal, muscular and neurological systems, are added to the children's repertoire. Once they begin to walk there are significant changes in the quality of the walking movement. As Thomas, Lee and Thomas (1988: 39) point out 'At first, walking is a stagger from place to place. It involves taking risks as balance is alternatively lost and re-established as steps are taken'. Eventually, those children who are secure and 'at home' in their newly acquired locomotive skills show a high degree of confidence, and associated emotional stability, detected in the easy and unrestricted way in which they move. There will be other children who may be able to walk but who move in a disjointed and less fluid way. Usually all that is needed at this early stage is help to achieve greater fluency and 'togetherness' although the walk of some children with learning difficulties is frequently characterised by disjointedness or lack of bodily cohesion. Additional time and commitment spent on this phase now is a good investment for the future as the ability to move around freely, and at will, provides fresh opportunities to explore the environment. Adding walking to standing brings about another vast extension of learning experiences. A consideration of these and other environmental experiences will be looked at in greater depth in Chapter 4.

Running

In terms of progression it is not such a far cry from walking to running, an activity which often emerges within the domain of a playful game. Excitement and eagerness to get to an enticing object or situation such as a hand proffering a toy or to get away from Father in 'friendly pursuit', may well provide the necessary stimulus to 'run'. Zaichkowsky, Zaichkowsky and Martinek (1980: 39), describing this initial pattern as a hurried walk point out:

> *This is not a genuine run, since the child does not have sufficient balance or leg strength to allow both feet to leave the ground momentarily.*

Eventually, locomotion develops into the 'genuine run' referred to here during which children incorporate a brief moment of flight into their action. This is a significant development which, because of the initial brevity of being airborne, is sometimes overlooked. As legs become stronger so the length of the stride increases, replacing the rise and fall features of the earlier action. The use of the arms changes character too. Unfocused, roundabout pathways become straight backwards-forwards ones which now occur in opposition to the movement of the legs. With an easy and smooth action in place children around five or six years are into real running. At this stage the action schema is extended through notions of speed, distance and endurance; how fast, how far and for how long. Just as early stages of walking involve instances of tottering and falling, early stages of running often result in grazed knees and bloody noses! The establishment of walking and running behaviour is welcomed by parents and educators alike as significant in the learning continuum.

Photograph 20   Mark, aged six years, runs with ease

Development at different rates

It is important to remember that at this stage a minority of children may show signs of some degree of impairment or delay in their motor development, sometimes referred to as clumsiness. Should such diagnosis be made, specialist help should be sought early on. The medical research charity, Action Research (1994), published a leaflet of advice to parents with children suffering from dyspraxia, the name given to this co-ordination disorder. Among other symptoms, attention is drawn to problems of balance and movement co-ordination which diminish ability to cope with everyday life. Referring to the 'hidden' disorder of a clumsy child, the report suggests that as many as 5 to 10 per cent of children fall into this category. This supports the earlier findings of Groves (1989) who indicated that 5 per cent of children at school experience motor problems and that there is likely to be at least one 'physically awkward' child in every primary school class. In a different context, and with reference to the visually impaired, Nielsen (1992: 43) draws attention to the ways in which gross motor activity such as that seen in running is replaced. She writes:

Instead of experimenting with how far and how fast it is possible to run and instead of preferring running to walking, many blind children fulfill their need for gross motor activity by jumping on the same spot or by experimenting with tiptoeing.

Balance adjustment

As children continue to explore their environment we see that balancing adjustments are called for time and time again – when carrying an ice cream, turning a corner, balancing along a wall, walking on icy roads or trying out something new. Photograph 21 shows the way in which Hannah, aged four, 're-adopts' the use of her arms as she manoeuvres the ball with her feet. Notice, too, the direct focus on her activity and the signs of bound flow which is frequently present when children try out new activities.

While a comfortable and effective level of dynamic balance is essential for the movement development of all children there is no doubt that some are better at balancing feats than others and display a particular and ongoing interest in this aspect of movement expertise. Sometimes, these children go

Photograph 21 Arms come into play when new balancing skills are needed

on to exploit their particular interest or skill in terms of recreational, amateur or professional settings. In physical activities such as skateboarding, ice-skating, skiing, rock-climbing and acrobatics, a reduced base for balance and the need to adapt to a changing environment are constant challenges. Such interests, either in terms of active participation or as a spectator sport, often become lifelong pursuits and in these, just as in earlier stages of balance, the kinaesthetic sense, 'knowing by a bodily feel', is constantly in evidence.

Throwing

Throwing is a complex activity in which several parts of the body move simultaneously as they cope with the release and propulsion of an object of some kind. Like balancing, throwing is an early activity in the behaviour of babies and, similarly, as a developed skill, is used in a variety of lifelong situations. The order of skill acquisition in this action is progressive but the amount of time it takes to achieve a fluent and effective action varies with individual children.

Early throwing pattern

In the earliest attempts to throw, the action starts mainly at the elbow with the body facing the direction in which the throw is to take place. The weight of the child's body at the point of release is either forward or backward, usually forward. The trunk is flexed and there is usually very little body adjustment happening during the action. To throw you also need the ability to 'let go' and this is something that takes time to develop. Observation of a two-year-old feeding ducks in the local pond provides a good example of what is meant here. With careful precision a young girl, aged about two years, pulled a fairly large piece of bread from a bag and with a forward projectory movement threw it into the pond near to where she was standing. She had some difficulty in releasing the bread at the appropriate moment in space and time and it dropped almost straight down – getting nowhere near the ducks! After the throw had been achieved her fingers remained taut and extended for several moments before the whole procedure was repeated. This throwing pattern was similar to the one in Photograph 22 which shows Laura, aged two-and-a-half, who has just thrown some gravel from one part of the path to another.

Same arm, same leg

A major difference in overarm throwing with slightly older children is indicated by the way the whole body begins to show early signs of co-ordinated action. The arm is swung diagonally backward and the elbow is flexed although the trunk usually remains facing front. As the throwing action takes place the body weight either remains on two feet or a forward step is taken on the same side as the throwing arm. The fingers are not necessarily extended at the moment of release and the throwing arm usually continues its arc downward and forward. Underarm throwing also features prominently in young children as shown by William in Photograph 23. He is well co-ordinated and his 'same arm, same leg' stance is typical of three-year-olds.

The technique of throwing matures

When the technique of throwing matures, fluent and effective co-ordination of the body is marked. For example, as the throwing arm is swung backward in preparation so the body rotates and the other arm is raised in complementary balance. With the weight of the body on the back foot the whole body is in a state of articulate preparation. From here the throw is achieved with a strong, spatially directed movement accompanied by a forward step on the opposite foot. Although his weight is not completely taken on his back foot Benjamin, aged seven, shown in Photograph 24 demonstrates the maturing of skilled action well.

The importance of throwing and catching

Throwing and catching are essential ingredients of children's play. The mastery of these twin activities provides access to endless hours of solitary and group play of both a collaborative and competitive nature. It is worthwhile to spend time and imagination in providing the right sorts of experiences at appropriate times in order for children to have a good initiation in this area of movement. Some children will excel in this type of activity and proceed to make games a major interest in their lives needing little more at first than apparatus and friends in the way of external motivation. However, a basic proficiency in these activities is the right of all children if they are to take part alongside their peers without the fear of being singled out as someone who cannot throw or catch and, consequently, left out of the game and the

Photograph 22   Early throwing pattern ending with outstretched hand

Photograph 23   Same arm, same leg – a typical throwing action

Photograph 24   The throwing technique matures

camaraderie which accompanies it. There will be a comfortable time later on when children can rationalise their own wishes to opt out of games for good reasons of their own. To be able to do this from the level of a basic competence is far better than for reasons of inadequacy.

Arnold (1988: 128) identifies throwing, catching and balancing as examples of 'pre-requisite skills'. He describes a person unable to kick, trap, dribble and pass as someone unable to participate successfully in soccer, a game where such skills are fundamental ingredients. There is no doubt about the authenticity of this claim and many instances of reluctance on the part of the children to 'join in' games can be traced to non-existent or low-level skills. In identifying distance and deviance in the context of play and the culture of childhood, Brown (1994: 61) comments that:

> *the ability to operate successfully within the society of children can be seen to depend upon performance in play and its associated activities.*

From the children's point of view, feelings of ineptitude are made worse by the knowledge that their presence in a team eager for a lively and effective game, and perhaps a victory, is unwelcome. Brown goes on to refer to this sense of rejection felt by children who are isolated when their performance of a chosen activity is judged unsatisfactory by a group.

Although what Arnold claims is in no doubt we should remember that, in the first instance, what are called 'prerequisite skills' exist in the form of singular or co-ordinated skills in their own right. At this early stage they are not prerequisites for anything more than responding to immediate challenges posed by the environment or self. The emergence and development of basic skills are evident in a variety of activities in which young children engage in the first eight years of life and for which they show a considerable appetite.

A young appetite for movement

Children have a natural appetite for movement, an appetite which requires as much consideration and attention as their appetites for food, drink, rest and sleep. We have only to walk onto a beach, enter a park, wait at a bus stop or be anywhere in the company of young children, to sense what is meant by movement being a common denominator of all activity and a 'must' in their lives. Wherever our gaze rests, young children can be observed demonstrating their natural interest in moving, their physical need and motivation to move. The frequency and intensity may vary but the nature and purpose of the activity remain constant factors. To deny, or seriously restrict, opportunities for children to move is now a relatively rare occurrence but where it happens the results are predictable and sad. The interest that young children display in moving falls into four distinct but interrelated categories:

- relating their bodies to *the stable environment* through such actions as *clambering, climbing, swinging, and balancing*
- testing themselves in terms of strength and *acrobatic and athletic mobility* as they *roll, tumble, leap and land*
- testing themselves in terms of dexterity through *handling and playing with objects* such as *rattles, balls, hoops, ropes, sticks, conkers and stones*
- *enjoying movement for its own sake* in the *turning, spinning, twirling, swooping activities* which appear spontaneously from time to time.

Movement activity related to the stable environment

Movement in this category is related to the relatively permanent features of the physical environment where young children gain experience, knowledge and understanding of their immediate surroundings and of themselves. They climb people, furniture and household features such as stairs and steps, graduating to railings, fences and trees. They balance along the edges of carpet, kerbstones and walls, swing round banisters, lamp-posts and overhanging branches of trees, somersault over traffic barriers and jump on, off, over and round anything and everything in sight. It is interesting to observe that even situations which might appear to adults to be inappropriate, uninspiring or even barren for the pursuit of movement are perceived quite differently by children – by Jane for example.

Jane, aged two, was the only child at a small family picnic in Richmond Park. The picnic spot was away from trees and water and, being flat, offered no opportunities for tumbling and rolling. As her family talked together, the only thing for Jane to play with was her own pushchair. For half an hour Jane used this as her personal climbing frame to step on, climb, balance, twist, turn and jump from. The pushchair, which she normally associated with transporting her, and in which her activity was restricted, had now become a stimulus for movement. Jane's prolonged period of activity showed a wide variety of action schemas being performed on one object.

This use of a variety of schemas was also typical of Amandip's situation, although his performance was more advanced and his zone of activity larger. Amandip, aged seven, found the four steps with a handrail at one side, leading to the front of his grandmother's house, a haven of experimentation. The 'domestic playground' presented endless possibilities for running, jumping, hanging, swivelling and swinging. He set himself increasingly difficult challenges which, when mastered, were shown and explained with pride to the family gathering before he set off again on the next round of self-challenging feats. From time to time his aunt took photographs of the latest activities and these no doubt provided 'fodder' for his next experiments.

The mobile and acrobatic use of the body

From early on young infants spend time using their bodies to bend, stretch, twist, turn and roll in a seemingly endless variety of ways. Sometimes this is for a specific purpose, such as reaching for an object. At other times it is for no reason at all other than for bodily and rhythmic satisfaction. As children become secure in altering their stance and positions at will so a much wider experimentation canvas is available to them. They try out their bodies in self-chosen, inventive feats of strength, mobility, dexterity and speed and young children can be seen rolling down grassy slopes, attempting to take weight on their hands, walking upside-down on all fours and jumping high and far across real or imagined obstacles. For hours on end such play takes place, sometimes satisfying personal goals but often caught up in group activity where everyone is pursuing the same or similar ends.

Photographs 25–28 of Mark, aged six, presuppose many hours of experimenting and self-assessment. Much time was spent putting his hands on the floor, crouching down and tucking in his head, and letting his weight take over before achieving that much longed for sequence of movement officially known as a somersault or forward roll – and by Mark as a 'roly-poly'. As a result of his practice Mark has achieved a fluidity and fluency of movement that demonstrates seamless transitions between the different parts of the activity. However, Mark is a highly co-ordinated boy who is interested and able in a wide range of movement activities and not all children will achieve this level of expertise so early.

Commenting upon the complexity of a forward roll Maude (1996: 200) informs us that it involves at least seventeen flexions and extensions of joints. She outlines detailed progressions leading up to the final outcome for children who are less confident. However, while such stepping stones may be

Photographs 25–28
Putting the parts together: a forward roll

generally helpful we should remember there are some children who actively dislike movement which requires a momentary loss of equilibrium and may not want to try out activities of this kind. It is important that in such cases children are not pressurised into doing so.

Handling objects and making them move

This area of movement activity probably represents the largest proportion of a young child's movement play. The gripping, shaking, releasing, dropping and throwing of toys, and other assorted objects, are well-known phenomena of young behaviour. Even early signs of 'team play' may be detected in the way in which an adult is actively involved in picking up a toy from the floor so that the game of dropping or throwing may take place again and again! *Setting things in motion, keeping things in motion and stopping things in motion* are dominant movement schemas of early childhood and provide delight for most children involved in such activities. The quantity of handling experience which children seek for themselves is a reflection of their seemingly insatiable appetite for movement of this type. Wherever they happen to be they always find something 'at hand' or 'at foot' to activate. Such appetites linger on, for the empty drink can on the path and the pebble on the shore lure the hands and feet not only of children but also of accompanying adults!

Although handling activities appear early in childhood, they take longer to develop than the first two groups of movement activity. This is due to dependence upon the development of motor skills and eye–hand/eye–foot co-ordination as well as immature concepts of space and time. But far from putting this type of activity to one side it is all the more important to provide a wide range of appropriate experiences as early as possible. If children in the Foundation Stage have handled objects of different weights, lengths and sizes – pebbles, balls, sticks, bats and ropes – they are more likely to cope with the activities and games lessons at Key Stages 1 and 2. Although a three-year-old may not be able to receive and hit a ball thrown by an adult, a game where a ball is directed, almost placed, on to the bat is meaningful not just as a preparation for 'real games' to be experienced in the junior school, but as a spontaneous here and now game of fun and for getting into the swing of things.

John, aged six, provides us with an interesting example in Photograph 29. While on holiday he was trying his hand at shooting into a net attached to

Photograph 29   The release of functional action into expressive behaviour

a pole. It was one of two nets placed at different heights to allow for varying skill maturation. As he walked across to the play area with his father and friends, John commented that he had managed to get the ball into the lower net seven times the day before and into the higher net once. He then proceeded to practise shooting at the lower net again while his father used the higher one. John watched his father bending his knees and 'lining up' his body as he prepared to 'shoot', observations which John then incorporated into his own shots. This was a productive situation where John practised his own game alongside his father while exchanging 'in context' talk as they went along. Having scored a goal, John was delighted with his success and, as we can see, released the narrow alignment of his body taken up while shooting into a wide expressive gesture.

The expressive use of the body

Sometimes, young children do not seek the challenge of exploring the stable environment, performing acrobatic tricks or making things move, but instead choose to engage in movement for its own sake and to use it expressively. In the very young it may be seen in the waving, beating and shaking of arms; in slightly older children the equally spontaneous activities of gliding, leaping, whirling, swirling and fluttering. Children may show anger when misunderstood, gentleness when looking after 'the patient' while excitement of any kind can make them shiver, shake or gesticulate excitedly. Children spinning together for the sheer enjoyment of the sensation it gives, moving to music being played, or donning a crown and 'becoming' a princess are all examples of children's expressive movement. Sometimes they join in with the rhythmic breaking of the waves on the shore or the sound of a car as it takes a bend at speed. Such activities are the stuff of dance and, as such, form the basis of dance experiences given at home, in statutory education or during classes in the local dancing school.

The movement curriculum in early childhood education

This fourfold classification of activities, in which young children frequently engage of their own free will represents the informal and formal movement curriculum associated with early childhood settings and which, ideally, extends and structures learning of this kind. The children's climbing, swinging and balancing activities find their place, along with their acrobatic skills, within gymnastics. Early experiences in making objects move are developed further in games and athletics while the children's expressive movement is catered for in dance. The differentiated provision made for movement education of all kinds is of the utmost importance. It is only when early learning experiences are matched and extended with appropriately challenging provision that we can hope to achieve the best possible movement heritage for our children.

The responses of very young children

For very young children the lines between the separate types of activities are blurred and the responses they make to external structures and the structure of their own bodies are complex. Whitehead (1990: 115) gives a movement-stressed example of a small child dragging chairs into a line and calling them a train while simultaneously enjoying the physical pleasure of climbing on and off them. A similar example, but one which this time starts with movement itself, is of a four-year-old girl who, wearing a 'yachting' cap, climbs to the top of the frame where she operates as the captain, looking out to sea, while organising her crew below. She enjoys the activity of climbing which enables her to reach the 'lookout' as well as the dramatic play which follows. This experience straddles the functional activity of climbing and the expressive play associated with being captain, and it is difficult to know which of these concerns prompted the other. In essence, they belong totally together as a unique experience which Whitehead (1990: 17) describes in this way:

> *Symbolic activities are particularly interesting for the early-years educator because they are the fusion of the unique personal experiences and concepts of the individual with the shared systems of shared meanings specific to the culture.*

Summary

Attention has focused on ways in which children physically manage their bodies in tandem with accompanying areas of their development. A range of activities characterising their natural appetite for movement has been identified through which their evolving movement vocabulary is extended. Following the assumption that the development of movement requires as much consideration and knowledge as other aspects of early learning, subsequent chapters will look at appropriate provision and enablement.

3

Moving to learn

Movement gives young children kinaesthetic feedback. This means that they link movement and learning through their senses.

(Bruce and Meggitt 2002: 66–7)

Notions of *moving and thinking* and *moving and feeling* are perhaps less familiar and accessible than links between movement and physical development. The main purpose of this chapter, therefore, is to identify ways in which movement is inextricably linked with *cognitive* (intellectual) and *affective* (emotional) functioning by looking at selected activities carried out by children and analysing them with reference to key educational theories. It is based on the premise that movement permeates the complex process of early growth and development, contributing to the physical, cognitive, emotional and social aspects of young lives. Movement belongs to them all and they belong to each other. The way in which they are viewed or presented at any given time is mainly a matter of emphasis.

Action, feeling and thought

In Chapter 1 attention was drawn to a lack of available resources and guidelines for the recognition and nurture of early movement development in comparison with those related to literacy, numeracy and science. As we turn now to look at ways in which movement is linked with cognitive, emotional and social functioning a similar lack of support can be found. This is not the case in some early childhood literature where well-known and prestigious writing includes movement alongside other areas of learning: Athey (1990), Bruce (1996, 1997), Dowling (2000) and Matthews (2002). There are also some more generalised cases made for the recognition of the important part movement plays in cognitive development and these should not be underestimated. A number of curriculum-oriented books include physical education within their brief, although it is interesting to note the tendency for these particular chapters to appear at or near the end of the book whatever stage of statutory education is being considered.

In its suggestions for developmentally appropriate practice for children aged between five and eight years, the National Association for the Education of Young Children (NAEYC 1992) claims that physical activity is vital for children's cognitive growth. They stress the need for physical actions to help them grasp abstract concepts. Engagement in active rather than passive activities is emphasised by Katz and Chard (1989) as an important underlying principle of primary education. Both the NAEYC and Katz and Chard imply a concern for what is considered valuable in terms of education. More recently, *The National Curriculum: Handbook* (DfEE and QCA 1999) and the QCA's *Physical Education: Teacher's Guide* (QCA and DfEE 2000) write at some length about what distinguishes work at different levels and the anticipated content in different subject units. While these documents indicate what teachers might expect in terms of physical education components and suggest ways in which activities and skills develop, there is nothing written about how these activities relate to developmental theories and why they are placed as they are.

In much of the literature which might help to pursue the intrapersonal and interpersonal issues considered in this book references to associated cognitive and movement development are relatively rare. Compared with other areas of learning little has been written in respect of specific concepts and schema. Once again movement appears as the poor relation. General characteristics of thinking can be identified in a wide variety of subjects such as art, drama, music, science and language and, therefore, it is difficult to understand why movement features so little in educational texts. This is especially the case as the language used in identification of schema in other subjects is often movement oriented.

However, the role of 'action' in relation to 'thought' has been central in some recent significant literature, Athey (1990) and Carter (1998), since Piaget (1971: 139) defined thought as internalised action when he wrote:

> *The life of the mind is a dynamic reality and intelligence a real and constructive activity.*

Zaichkowsky, Zaichkowsky and Martinek make a case that through movement and play children learn more than motor skills. They suggest that children:

- learn to employ cognitive strategies
- understand themselves in psychological terms
- learn how to interact with other children (Zaichkowsky, Zaichkowsky and Martinek, 1980: 11).

In attempting to establish cognitive development within the sphere of movement, where possible, examples will be related to literature which encapsulates, extends and appropriately sites the work of Piaget. In spite of recent reservations about Piaget's work, modified adherence to his theories is expressed by many educationalists such as Athey (1990), Bruce (1987, 1991, 1997), Matthews (2002), Nutbrown (1994) and Roberts (2002). However, in relating movement to stages of cognitive development, and in referring to specific concepts, there is no intention to 'force a fit' with Piaget's work. It is clear that leading educationalists and movement specialists know that movement goes hand in hand with developmental theory and the instances they cite are relevant and meaningful. The significant lack is in terms of hard evidence underlying the variety of beliefs and claims, and in the articulation of specific and substantial links with current educational and psychological theory.

A research project

Before considering specific concepts within children's movement activities it may be helpful to look at a piece of early research carried out to investigate whether stages of cognitive development could be identified through movement (Davies 1976). It was found that children between the ages of five and eleven years were able to see similarities (classify), order differences (seriate) and compose in movement reflecting the stages put forward by Piaget (1953). The findings also suggested that children not only reached these stages but that, by using movement based on their own experiences, they did so earlier than with the traditional test material featuring shape, size and colour.

As part of the research programme, and of particular relevance here, was a movement test which was designed to investigate children's ability, at the ages of five, seven and eleven years, to carry out the following:

- to invent an activity based on given activities
- to repeat it
- to hold it in mind while describing it

- to dissect it
- to reverse it.

Setting up the programme

Climbing, balancing and jumping were chosen as the movement ingredients for the test. These were known to be within the capabilities of all the subjects and were recognised as the three most commonly used actions of children between five and eleven years old. Further safeguards included a visit by all the children to a common venue where they experienced all three actions and observed them being carried out by a student. The children were then asked to make up an activity where there was some balancing, some jumping and some climbing and to make it something they could do over and over again. While this test was formally conducted for research purposes, it was based on, and carried out through, 'child-familiar' activities – activities defined by Bruce (1987: 135) as embedded in meaning.

The programme in action

After they had time to become acclimatised to the situation in which they were working, and to make up their activities, the children were individually asked to talk about them in the following ways:

- to describe them without looking at the apparatus
- to comment on isolated parts of their activity and to select parts from the whole
- to reverse the order of their actions.

General findings showed that there were significant differences between the three age groups and no difference between the achievements of boys and girls.

First, the children were asked in the absence of the apparatus to describe their activity and this presented some problems for nearly all the five-year-olds. Seated at a table facing the tester and with their backs to the apparatus, nearly all the younger subjects turned round to look at the specific place where their activity had taken place in order to give an answer. Even when at a later stage, with the apparatus in full view this time, they were asked for a description, several of them got up from their chair, approached the apparatus and, in some cases, touched it. This illustrated a need to identify the movement context visually in order to recall with accuracy. In turning to look at the specific place where they had been working, or making physical contact through touch, the younger children seemed to be 're-visiting' the familiarised context which made 'human sense to them' (Donaldson 1978: 25).

The next questions the children were asked referred to their ability to:

- look at parts of their activity in relation to other parts
- describe what came before or after something else
- describe how it all began
- describe how it came to an end.

Carrying their actions in their heads and selecting passages at will, as well as illustrating thought after internalised action, appeared within the grasp of the majority of seven- and eleven-year-olds, while only a few of the five-year-olds came near to this level of functioning.

The final test of mentally reversing their actions, that is, starting with their last action and tracing their actions backwards to the beginning, found a drop of a third in the seven-year-old range. This is difficult to equate with their earlier success. However, on reflection, it might be argued that the movements and their transitions which made up their various activities had a natural flow from one to the next which lost their inherent logic in reverse order. The movement feeling, or in Donaldson's terms, 'the sense', was lost. It is similar to the rewinding of a film or video tape where the sense or the meaning becomes divorced from the original context.

Analysing the results

The first tentative implication of this study is that information concerning cognitive development appears in movement, where children use their bodies as a major framework of reference, before other more established contexts external to children such as blocks. This discovery signals an important additional dimension to the movement component of early childhood education and care. Since this piece of research was carried out the notion of a fixed and developmental order in the acquisition of logical operations has been challenged and accordingly modified. The important issue now is to examine relevant notions of movement-related cognition in the light of current educational theory.

Immediately following the completion of the research study the children were asked to paint about their climbing, balancing and jumping activities. It was found that degrees in accurate and detailed verbal description, which was already shown to correspond to the detail and complexity of their movement activity, corresponded with the children's ability to represent their three actions pictorially (Photographs 30, 31 and 32). It is interesting to see the way the children have 'composed' their paintings to give the picture 'as they see it'. Matthews (1994) draws attention to the important role that composition plays in young children's paintings and makes the point that it is not an optional affair.

The five-year-olds

Mandy's painting indicates a clear differentiation of activity. The act of jumping is indicated by the space she has left between the two boxes and, although balancing does not show her feet in contact with the bench, the outstretched arms give important information about what is going on. Climbing is less immediately distinguishable although there is some indication of the vertical uprights of the climbing frame and, therefore, the up-down direction in which the activity takes place.

Luke's painting shows much clearer representation. The action of balancing indicates both feet in contact with the bench and arms are helping too. In the representation of jumping we see that the body is clearly in front of the box over which the leap has taken place. There can be little doubt that this is Luke's favourite activity. Climbing, again proving to be the most difficult action to convey, is communicated partly through the vertical and horizontal structure of the climbing frame.

Alison's painting shows a similar representation to Luke's. Outstretched arms and firmly planted, 'footless legs', indicate balancing while a space between the 'footless legs' and bench clearly indicate jumping. It is interesting to note the absence of arms in this action which could be interpreted as being less important and, by their omission here, emphasise their use in balancing. Climbing is well expressed in the case of the frame but Alison places her body in front of it, almost merging with it. As Alison continues with 'sorting out' projective space in visual representation she should soon be able to represent herself from the back.

Photograph 30
Mandy's painting

Photograph 31
Luke's painting

Photograph 32
Alison's painting

The seven year olds

The next two paintings (Photographs 33 and 34) resemble more closely the activities as they were executed. The 'sophistication' in comparison with the three previous paintings is clear.

Photograph 33   Joanna's painting

Photograph 34   Mark's painting

In contrast to the paintings of the five-year-olds, all three activities in Joanna's painting show the body facing a different, and appropriate, direction. The use of hands and feet, more detailed here, all show relevance. We see her 'pushing off' the stool in jumping, 'attached to' the bench in balancing, and 'gripping' the rope in climbing. The articulated knee joints are also worthy of note and add to the 'movement feel'. It is interesting to speculate at this stage of 'visual realism' whether experiential activity – that is, carrying out the activities themselves – together with more highly developed observational skills may have helped towards the clarity seen in this painting.

The experiential probability is especially relevant to Mark's painting. For example, the use of the arms is differentiated in some detail. The regulatory, two-dimensional position gives an impression of striving to maintain balance while the more mobile expression of the arms suggests flight of a more fluid nature. There is an expression of feeling in this painting which is referred to by Ives (1984: 152–9) as 'content expression'. With Mark's hair standing on end, and the implied height of the jump through its placement in relation to the other activities in the picture, we are led to believe that this is an exciting experience. While climbing is shown in a rather static, symmetrical pose, distance and perspective are all in evidence and, unlike the paintings of the five-year-olds, the body is shown facing the 'well-remembered' design of the climbing frame.

The next step

Some interesting information arises from this research, and associated continuation studies, in terms of cognitive development and links with movement. What is most needed now is information which relates to specific movement activities and the schematic development of these in early childhood learning. With this in mind this chapter is primarily concerned with the place and importance of movement as a common denominator of the development of thinking.

Movement and spatial schema

The number and refinement of interdependent actions which children possess at any given time is partly reflected in the spatial use of their bodies in the environment in which they move. Gerhardt is almost exclusively concerned with ways in which young boys and girls oriente themselves in space. Through her many detailed examples she shows how body movement is recognised as an underlying and essential component of children's learning. She writes:

> *Body movement is the foundation of thought. It derives from, and contributes to, sensory perception, imagery and thought. Each human being organizes his experiences into his own patterns. These patterns become his unique frame of reference in which, and through which, he assimilates new data.*
>
> (Gerhardt 1973: 12)

When young children balance along walls, climb over gates, jump over streams and activate see-saws they are developing notions of space. Through these, and a variety of associated actions, they come to know about such things as strength, flexibility, height, width, distance and proximity. Spatial knowledge which comes about when children respond to the environment in this active way is an important part of learning and a good one to start with here.

Observing Kriss at play: a structured environment

The following activities were observed in a play area for young children over a period of twenty minutes. Three-year-old Kriss was one of many children enjoying the facilities in his local park. He was well co-ordinated and rhythmical in his movement and extremely agile in the activities he carried out. However, on this particular occasion, the main point of interest was on the *spatial use of his body and the consequent learning taking place.* Although the level of Kriss's activity was intense it was mainly restricted to two particular sections of agility apparatus to which he kept returning. In both these situations his concentration focused on three spatial components, namely, '*up*', '*down*' and '*through*'.

Climbing up the scrambling net and sliding down the pole was an activity repeated time and time again, always with a pause at the top platform before making his descent. 'I'm a fireman,' he said, 'they have to get there quickly.' On all counts it was clear that Kriss climbed up in order to slide down – the favourite part of his activity (Photograph 35). He soon realised that in order to enjoy his favourite sliding bit he had to climb to the right height. The climbing and sliding actions carried out in relation to the scrambling net and

Photograph 35 *'Being a fireman' sliding down the pole*

the pole brought into play a complex set of schemas. Later when this activity became sufficiently well established he gave it symbolic meaning. He demonstrated his knowledge that firemen had to move quickly and that this involved sliding down poles.

Choosing a ladder and adjoining chute Kriss found a second situation in which to make a sliding descent. This activity he also repeated many times. The passage to his starting place at the bottom of the ladder was often obstructed by other children. At first, rather than take an alternative and sometimes shorter route, he stuck to his original circuit in spite of the obstructions he met and the time it took to get there. Having climbed the ladder he sometimes found the entrance to the chute already in use and had

Photograph 36   Waiting for a turn – out of sight but not out of mind

to wait his turn. On these occasions, he couldn't see his father waiting for him at the bottom of the chute because other children were having their turn. Nevertheless, he called out 'Wait for me, I'm coming' (Photograph 36).

In addition to the *up-down dimension*, the two alternating activities which Kriss pursued have two other things in common. One is the climbing action preceding the descent and the other is the type of descent. In both instances this involved a sensation element of the body being 'taken over' in response to its own weight. However, although the descent had things in common, there were two significant differences. Once positioned at the top of the chute, the release of his hands was all that was needed to set Kriss's body in motion for the downward journey. This was less demanding in terms of physical exertion than the 'fireman's slide' where the hands had to grip the pole.

Another glance at the photograph of Kriss coming down the pole shows that at this stage he does not use his feet in order to take some of the weight of his body although there is some attempt to position them appropriately. The considerable bodily demands in using the pole in this way may have had something to do with the pause Kriss made at the top each time as if preparing himself for the descent. The difficulty involved may also have prompted the periodic change Kriss made from this activity to the other.

Although there were two conventional slides in the play area Kriss did not choose to go on either of these, although they were sometimes free. This may have been because the secondary spatial idea, prominent in his exploratory play, was '*going through*' and, therefore, the chute which is enclosed like a tunnel was more relevant to this spatial schema than the slides which were open-sided and open-topped. On one occasion when his selection of 'going through' spaces were completely occupied Kris looked round and called to his father 'I know, I know where I can go' (meaning 'I know where else I can do it') and proceeded to leave the play area and run to an adjacent field where a stile led from one side to the other. Using the step which connected the two sides to squeeze himself 'through the gap', he proudly demonstrated his new activity.

Kriss was talking to himself as he went about his two activities and at intervals he also verbalised his actions to his father and friends. His language was almost entirely related to what he was doing, with frequent references to his body and where movement was happening in terms of its spatial location. Accompaniment of the activities with verbalisation is an important ingredient of cognitive development for Kriss, for as Gerhardt (1973: 31) points out 'Words preserve actions through time. They label and thus generate experience'. His father played an active part in the conversational exchange, making the time spent together not only a companionable occasion but also an educative experience.

Calvin suggests that we have a passion for stringing things together and suggests that structured strings might be a core activity of the brain useful for language, storytelling, planning ahead, games and ethics. He writes:

> *Besides words into sentences, we combine notes into melodies, steps into dances, and elaborate narratives into games with procedural rules.*

(Calvin 1997: 95)

In Kriss's case the stringing together was twofold, movement and words, the schematic handling complex and therefore all the more significant.

From this twenty-minute movement exploration, which included many separate, spatially oriented activities often experienced by young children in similar settings, we turn to three further specific examples of moving and knowing.

The department store: an unusual play environment

The next example of children thinking through movement while exploring a stable environment features Nicola, aged three years, who discovered an empty clothes rail while her aunt was paying her bill in a department store. It was an ordinary, orthodox kind of rail with lower and upper horizontal bars between two quite sturdy uprights. Nicola had established an activity around the bottom rail and one of the uprights, saying aloud this sequence to herself as she moved:

> *under and over*
> *under and over*
> *under and over*
> *round and round and round and round.*

Both the activity itself, and the words she used to describe it, clearly establish this as a predominantly spatially stressed activity. However, as well as doing and verbalising, or rather as a result of it, Nicola had established an interesting rhythmic build-up with a decisive and impactive ending to the phrase. Unusual though this activity might appear within a fairly busy department store, it was a normal response for Nicola to investigate what was immediately at hand. Having confirmed that no one was being inconvenienced or disturbed by her niece's activities her aunt allowed it to happen and her lack of anxiety made for a stress-free shopping expedition. Nicola's happy engagement in making and repeating her new activity supports the notion put forward by Singer and Singer (1990: 63) that 'when children are able to play openly and freely they become good learners, developing their cognitive skills through the stepping stones of play'.

The supermarket: it's me that makes it happen

Another example of children thinking through movement comes from a supermarket where, inside the store, two children waited with their parents to be let into the shopping area. The girl, aged about three, was experimenting with how near to the electronically controlled gate she had to stand in order for it to open. With the encouragement of her older brother to 'go a bit further' or to 'get nearer to the gate' she gradually became aware of the exact spot she needed to reach in order to activate it. Her squeals of delight were shared by her parents and the quite lengthy queue which had formed. While welcoming her success, the now completely involved onlookers were willing her to reach the next stage which was to understand that the gate would not close, and allow her to 'play the game' again, until she retreated from the point of activation. At this point her brother physically guided her away from where she stood helping her to make the gates close. However, it was clear from her expression that the 'success' in this instance lacked the essential understanding on her part. It was her brother's solution, kindly meant, not hers. She continued to experiment herself to find out just how far she had to advance or retreat to bring about the right response. In the end she succeeded, demonstrating thinking in terms of spatial, dynamic and relational aspects of movement. Above all, with or without her brother's help – and with support and shared delight from all around – it was fun. Both this activity and that of Nicola give information on how society values its children, and illustrates well many of the common principles identified by Bruce (1997: 16–17).

A height and depth of experience: adjusting the environment

The following example also demonstrates an appropriateness of action in relation to a stable environment, this time jumping and landing. It is more complex in nature than the previous ones and takes place in a group context. Although the spatial connotations are restricted to directions of *up and down*, the way in which these are extended and the consideration and reconsideration of the activity indicate a higher level of cognitive functioning.

A small group of boys, aged between four and six years, were jumping off a plank slotted into a climbing frame situated in the grounds of their school. After they had enjoyed this activity of jumping at the set height for some considerable time they took out the plank and inserted it one section higher. This happened several times and as the plank went up in height the boys had to climb further to reach it. There were three different reactions. Some boys continued to jump confidently from the newly established positions, some dropped out immediately knowing from experience that they had reached their 'personal best' while a few walked to the end of the plank and decided at the last moment whether or not to take off. In making a last-minute decision one boy expressed his thinking in words. He said '*It's higher now, it's too high to jump, there's further to drop*'. Through a successive sequence of events the boy had established a reference framework of jumping and landing. He connected the fact that he was 'higher' with having climbed up 'further' and therefore having a greater distance to drop. As part of this thought process he might also have been remembering the increasing lack of comfort, which accompanied each successive landing. It was this framework of experience, including feelings of pleasure and wariness, which became his guide to decision-making. It is interesting to note that although the climbing and jumping activity was essentially an individual one the children were, for the most part, working co-operatively alongside each other, involved in each other's efforts, watching and waiting upon events.

In essence, the children involved in this activity were constructing their own knowledge through a series of self-set challenges incorporating spatial notions, identified in Chapter 1.

- direction: up and down
- extension and size: big and little and near and far
- zones: above and below
- levels: high and low.

Although all these aspects of space were incorporated into the children's activity, it is interesting to note that one theme, namely *high and low*, was dominant with those of *extension, size and direction* being implied rather than emphasised. It is clear that the children were operating in different ways in this wide and complex area of cognitive functioning. On the whole the younger children concentrated on one or two things at a time, whilst the older ones were able to take several things into account. The boys who were considering whether to jump or not were able to reflect upon their experience and to make a decision in the light of it.

In addition to cognitive recognition of space there are clear indications in the boys' jumping activity of the concept of seriation or ordering which is about seeing the difference between things. In respect of seriation and classification (seeing similarities), Athey (1990: 41) writes:

Seriation and classification have their origins in early actions applied to a wide range of objects and, later, to events. The common-sense world contains sufficient information to feed seriation structures such as size, height, weight, strength, temperature, porosity, number and so on.

It is interesting to note that the first two seriation structures listed by Athey, namely *size and height*, have a place in the space section of the movement framework in Chapter 1. Also that her reference to *strength* relates to the dynamic notion of weight. As the boys were actively engaged in their jumping 'event' they could be said to be seriating their movement in the following ways:

- by positioning the plank increasingly higher up the frame
- by climbing higher at each turn
- by looking down from increasing heights
- by jumping from increasing heights.

Significantly, all these seriation components are associated with the children's major focus on level, ranging from high to low. The notion of high to low in this case was a personal as well as general notion – one boy's highest was different from that of another. A further example of the decreasing number of children 'left in' also has a seriation slant but this did not feature prominently until towards the end when only two boys were still taking part. We will return to children's ordering of movement activities later in this chapter after looking at some other activities showing how children learn through movement.

Children and objects in motion

As we saw, children learn in particular ways when they explore and challenge features of their natural and human-made environment. The learning experience is of a different kind when they handle objects and make them move at will. Finding out 'what I can do' with a particular object is a lengthy and absorbing area of behaviour which stretches from the explorations of babies right through to the professional games player. Children employ a range of basic actions in order to make objects move and to keep them moving. These include:

- grasping
- rolling
- sliding
- throwing
- catching
- striking
- propelling.

Photograph 37   Aaron, aged six years, tries out his games skills

Knowing 'how' to carry out these activities involves the 'thinking body' in dynamic action, making on-the-spot estimations based on lengthy periods of trying things out, of relating to elements of weight, size, shape and the movement properties of different pieces of apparatus. Photograph 37 shows Aaron, from Germany, experimenting with different ways of making contact with his football.

Self-made rules

Little has been said, so far, about the rules which govern games activity. In the first instance, rules are self-imposed boundaries that children place on their play and which they probably do not even regard as rules. The demand of a young child to '*Watch me, you see I have to stand behind this line and then throw it*' is an example of such self-made regulations. Often young children play their games in the same area as other children. This is either because a special time is set for the activity or because individual children join in naturally with the activities of those around them. Sometimes they share an idea. But only rarely before the age of about three years, do they 'share each other'. All the same, as they bowl their hoops or kick their balls they acquire a sense of other children taking part and being involved.

As children tip over into a more co-operative period they play at first with one other, gradually extending into small groups. Their own skill and love of activity remain dominant features; their association with other children is flexible and subsidiary and only a few rules bind them together. These rules, at first changeable and loose, arise from the restrictions and opportunities momentarily encountered. Coats serving as goal-posts, lines on the pavement indicating areas of play and conveniently placed trees denoting boundaries, all have a part to play in regulating 'the game'. So, too, do the procedures which govern their play. Times for changing over and taking on other roles, along with notions of supremacy, are mutually agreed. Because the rules and regulations are the children's own they understand them even if the adults to whom they are explained may have some initial difficulty!

Sometimes, play is affected by images from the professional world. For example, a common sight in football-type games, played by children as young as six, is the exultant leap into the air and an arm punching the air with triumph. The scoring of goals is often accompanied by cheers and hugs all round. As these expressive responses happen so often, and with such conviction, they must have a satisfying bodily feel as well as an identification with the professional game. The games play of five- and six-year-olds show other ways in which external models are there *in situ* but not necessarily integrated. Sometimes the children set up two goal areas and have two groups acting as teams. So far so good. However, often both teams play co-operatively and into one goal! At half-time, a time of their choosing, *all* players change over and play towards the other goal. The goalkeeper, if there is one, simply goes to the other goal area which, until this moment, has remained unused.

As games develop in skill and strategies and children make a transition into competitive games, so their involvement in the rules and regulations which govern their games increases. It is well known that at the top of the junior school such detail often hampers the actual playing of the game itself; it is a time when umpiring and reporting skills begin to take their place along with those of performance.

Appropriate provision

Some of the games-like equipment provided for children at home and in early childhood settings share common properties. For example, they can be made to travel along the ground and through the air in a variety of directions and with different degrees of force. However, individual pieces of equipment – balls, bean bags, hoops, quoits, bats, sticks – have special identity features of their own. At one time it was thought that a young child's selection of small apparatus was a random affair. We know now that this is unlikely to be the case. As Athey (1990: 41) points out children are continually searching for materials and experiences which will 'feed' their current stock of schemas. Examples of such feeding, that is the identification of movement-associated schemas, and appropriate provision to develop them, would take a longer time than this chapter permits. Therefore, just a few references to one piece of equipment, hoops, are included to suggest how this might be done.

Using hoops in play

Some of the special features of a hoop can be classified in this way:

- its circularity is continuous and enclosed.
- it remains the same shape whether it is lying on the floor, hanging on a storage peg or being held in the hand.
- it has an inside which is enclosed and space which surrounds it.
- it can surround and enclose the body, parts of the body and other objects.
- it can be rolled.
- it can be spun.

At first hoops may be used without any reference to their special properties. In common with any other objects feeding their transporting schema, very young children may simply carry them from place to place. Whalley (1994: 93) gives examples of ways transportation schema can be extended for the under-fives. Marcus, aged two, was one of a group of children aged between two and eleven years playing together. He carried his hoop around while watching the older children using theirs in a variety of different ways. Anxious to join in, it was at this moment that Marcus put his head through his hoop as captured in Photograph 38.

Photograph 38 Being enclosed

Eventually, children use hoops in relation to their specific features, the stage they have reached in their personal 'handling skills' and their own movement appetite. They send them rolling, and spin them on the ground, round their waists, arms and legs. They use them to jump into, out of, over and through. Later they become goals and target areas in solitary, co-operative and competitive games situations. At times they become racing cars, parachutes and traffic roundabouts as children engage in their symbolic play.

Families, friends and significant others: mother and daughter

Learning through movement goes on everywhere and not least of all in the home. In Photographs 39–41 we can see that three-year-old Harriet is experiencing a great deal of movement activity which carries bodily, dynamic, spatial and relational connotations. She is finding out that her body can do exciting, agile things. Expertly supported, and feet first, she goes up, over and down again – a backward somersault in the air. For the whole of the acrobatic journey she is passing through her mother's arms.

Photograph 39   Up

Photograph 40   Over

Photograph 41   And down

This, and similar agility activities may happen very quickly, in which case the continuity and flow are all-important. On other occasions, selected parts of the 'play game' can occur more slowly in order to emphasise what is taking place. Accompanying words from the mother such as *'Up you go'*, *'Over you go'* and *'Down you come'* will help to register the spatial significance of the various parts of the activity as they occur – words in which the children can also join.

This shared activity illustrates well the relationship category of movement first referred to in Chapter 1. The mother's role is appropriately supportive but Harriet is doing her bit too. She is working hard in terms of energy and her body is very active. Notice how her feet lead the way and how well placed they are. Her head goes backwards as her mother gently tips her to start her on her downward path. Harriet is clearly confident in this companionable play situation and her expression is one of fluency and ease. There needs to be mutual trust in movement activity of this sort as well as understanding of how to hold and to help. What a long way this mother and daughter play is from that of Sanna and Arne shown in Chapter 2.

Family games: brothers play together

Two brothers, Martin, aged eight and Graham, aged six, had set up a game for themselves, along the lines of cricket. All aspects of the game were related to what was available in terms of resources and their individual understanding at that time. In determining the length of the pitch it was agreed that they would measure this by a given number of strides. In terms of assessing how many of his strides would approximate to a reasonably accurate distance Martin took the lead and began measuring the pitch. But perceiving the situation from his point of view Graham warned him, saying, *'Not big steps because I can't bowl that far'*. Implicit in this comment was Graham's ability to relate Martin's length of stride to the distance to the proposed wicket. This, in turn, related to his own ability in bowling which was different from his brother's.

Friends compete: on their own terms

The remarkable amount of self-initiated interests in 'ordering activities' as seen in the boys' jumping and landing game often means going that bit further or finding another way of doing something. From an early stage children's movement activity is full of 'I can make what I am doing more difficult'. Later on, the challenge of 'I can do better than you' comes about. Competing to see who can put the most claps in between throwing a ball in the air and catching it is a simple illustration of what is meant here. To begin with, a group of very young children may take part in the contest without bothering to check who has won. This gradually develops to a time when one or more children are intent on getting the better of the others – to be 'the best'. A dance experience based on the theme 'Anything you can do I can do better' can be found in Chapter 8.

Two seven-year-old friends, Nasreen and Shanaz, incorporated the notion of difficulty into their activity. They made up a throwing and catching game in which the object was to throw the ball from one to the other with a penalty imposed every time it was dropped. The penalty scale which they agreed upon, and which rendered a player increasingly less effective, was along the following lines:

- one hand only to catch
- kneeling on one knee
- kneeling on two knees
- sitting down
- out.

If, while in one of these penalty positions, the ball was successfully caught, the player was allowed to return to the previous, more advantageous stage. In this way the players regained a hierarchical status in the reverse order of its loss. This game is a clear example of a traditional one which was modified to meet Shanaz's and Nasreen's needs. Competition of this kind has to do with increasing skill and maturity, and may relate to self-imposed goals, those traditionally handed down or a mixture of the two. Hierarchical variation in skipping is another example of increasing difficulty characterising competition with self and with others. The variations might be as follows:

- skipping forwards and backwards
- crossing the rope in front and behind
- 'doubles'
- skipping with a partner starting inside the rope
- skipping with a partner, running in
- skipping inside someone else's rope
- running in, skipping in someone's rope and running out.

Mark, aged six, can be seen in Photograph 42 starting out on his skipping schema. He knows he has to jump high in order to clear the rope and that the timing of the jump has to fit in with the way he controls the rope. In his efforts to co-ordinate jumping and rope-turning Mark's body has taken on an asymmetric design and his concentration has extended to his tongue!

Photograph 42   Mark can skip

A school setting

As a final example of children learning through movement we turn now to dance and specifically to the bonfire dance of a group of six- and seven-year-olds. At a certain point in the dance they had to work out how to arrive in a group – the central bonfire – coming from positions around the edge of the hall. Sometimes it worked well. Sometimes it was a muddle. It was never the same twice. It was difficult for some of the children to think ahead and imagine how others were solving the problems of contributing to the group shape and the nature of their contribution to the end outcome. As Blakemore

(2000: 6) suggests, an increased understanding of theory of mind, that is, knowing how someone else thinks, is characteristic of intellectual development in young children. However, this increasing ability to give, take and put themselves in the position of other children – in this case literally – needs practice. Help from the teacher can be useful in establishing some anchor points of first arrivals and then encouraging the others to find a place, perhaps joining at once, or waiting until a space becomes free.

Summary

Some of the ways children learn through movement have been looked at both generally and through detailed analysis of specific activities. The next chapter makes use of these observations as it considers a variety of learning and teaching environments appropriate to the movement education of early childhood.

4

The learning teaching environment

*Given an environment in which they are cared for and in which they can
thrive, young children display a range of competencies which make their early
learning dramatically successful.*   (Fisher 1996: 7)

This chapter considers how learning and teaching in its broadest sense can
be facilitated through appropriate environmental and teaching strategies. It
aims to connect the ideas set out in the previous three chapters and to suggest ways in which children can be helped to develop their movement potential and enhance their learning capacities. In doing so it acknowledges that
developing behaviour of any kind is dependent upon contributions from
both the child and the environment.

Making a good start

The importance of the right kind of environment is an early consideration of
parents even before birth takes place. An abundance of literature and advice
on such options as home births, hospital births, water births, births to music,
with or without partners being present, is available to guide decision-making
at this important time. From birth onwards young babies make sense of their
environment through what they see, hear, touch and smell and their sense
of movement. The interaction of the environment with sequential growth
and maturation throughout the first eight years of life is the nub of the educational process, a process which takes place at home and in all types of care
and educational settings. All situations in which children learn are important
and therefore it is vital that environmental provision is in position, and carefully considered, in every one of these.

McPherson, Curtis and Loy (1989) draw attention to a range of restraints
such as geography, topography and climate which inevitably limit a child's
experience of physical pursuits. However, although there are differences

between families or home units reflecting cultural, social and economic concerns it would seem that most of these are intent, right from the start, on providing as rich and supportive an environment as possible in order to extend spontaneous behaviour. The increasing use of specialised outlets such as Early Learning Centres, television programmes, play groups, library projects, and many other similarly designed initiatives, testifies to the high regard with which the majority of families hold opportunities for education and the associated 'good start in life'.

Supporting the view that parents do their best for their children's education Gillian Pugh and Erica De'Ath (1984: 169) write:

> *The great majority of parents are concerned to do their best for their children even if they are not always sure what this might be.*

There is a slight reservation in this statement which implies that, while there is a wish to help, there may be uncertainty about the form 'their best' should take. The QCA, while recognising the importance of the parent's role in educating their children, also recognise the need for them to be linked with professional practice and to be involved in partnership. They suggest:

> *Parents are children's first and most enduring educators. When parents and practitioners work together in early years settings, the results have a positive impact on the child's development and learning.*   (QCA 2000: 9)

In terms of movement, physical activity and young children seem to belong together – to go hand in hand and to be natural and valuable associates. Sometimes parents and early childhood practitioners take this to mean that the main purpose of provision is to encourage their children to be physically active, to let off steam and to keep fit. All these are commendable justifications and it would be foolish to deny the importance of aims associated with a sense of well-being, physical fitness and confidence. Most people would agree with Roberton and Halverson (1984: 11) that 'all children deserve the opportunity to become self-assured and competent in controlling their moving bodies'. But this is only part of the picture.

Learning and teaching: a movement-based environment

In what follows, the learning and teaching environment is related to specific categories of movement provision and to the developmental sequences reached by individuals and groups. As indicated in earlier chapters, children

Photograph 43 Bound flow accompanies new and difficult actions

Photograph 44 A new environmental challenge

will always find ways to explore their immediate environment. For example, we saw the two-year-old with her pushchair and Nicola's exploration of the clothes rail. Along with Lucy, aged three and Aaron, aged six, shown in Photographs 43 and 44, they also serve as examples of satisfying one particular movement appetite, in this case responding to challenges presented *by the stable features of the physical environment.*

In and around the home: natural and structured environments

Wherever children live, whether in houses, low-rise or high-rise flats, caravans, bed and breakfast accommodation, refuges or tents, play in proximity to home features prominently. Pedestrian walkways, 'no traffic' streets and reserved play spaces on housing estates all give regular access to railings, steps, walls and gates to stimulate agile activity. The immediacy and regularity of opportunity and experience provided by the local neighbourhood is enticing. Many children play in local haunts. However, if the immediacy and regularity of garden and street play are advantages, then the drawback lies in their unalterability. As Brierley (1987: 111) reminds us:

> *The brain thrives on variety and stimulation. Monotony of surroundings, toys that only do one thing, a classroom display kept up for too long, are soon disregarded by the brain.*

Most families with access to gardens provide climbing frames, swings, see-saws, clambering blocks, large boxes and tree houses for their children. However, it is important to keep in mind that, wherever possible, such agility units should reflect the developmental sequences of the children using it. This is not an easy task if the home unit contains two or more children below eight years of age. Equipment which differs in size, shape and proportions is an important consideration in the purchase and setting up of agility structures. Another thing to consider is whether it can be changed and modified in some way by children and adults, as in the 'furniture walkabout' and the boys who changed the level of the plank in their jumping activity discussed earlier. However, the in-built design features of much home- and school-based apparatus do not encourage change in its use. As a result, increased skill and versatility have to come from the children's own bodily inventiveness rather than from their response to the apparatus itself. Examples of child initiated exploration of this kind are numerous and include such things as:

- missing out alternate rungs when climbing to the top of the frame
- coming down the ladder without using the feet
- using the swing while standing instead of sitting
- jumping off the swing while it is still moving
- climbing up the chute instead of sliding down, resulting in a change of direction and action.

As suggested earlier, skilled movement in a safe and dependable setting, such as the garden or immediate neighbourhood, eventually needs to be experienced in an extended and less predictable context. All young members of the family can be taken on outings to parks, adventure playgrounds or the countryside where, according to their current developmental sequence, they can seek places to try out balancing feats, find stones and rocks to jump from and locate trees from which to climb and swing. All these activities reflect not only individual schematic-oriented interests but also any craze of the moment.

All I need is me – and sometimes you

Bodily agility without reference to structured apparatus is, in some ways, simpler to provide for and certainly less expensive. This is the time when children concentrate on finding out what their bodies will and will not do. Obviously, the garden, approaches to the home and flexible interiors are important here, especially if they incorporate grass, paved areas, slopes, steps, carpets and cushions – places where children can stand on their hands and their heads, run, roll and balance as they work towards their acrobatic and athletic potential.

As children respond readily to opportunities to carry out their acrobatic type of movement, tests of inventiveness and skill are developed in response to their own bodies as well as to 'models' passed on by, and shared with, family and friends. It is interesting to observe how generalised skilfulness gives way to set skills. Children discover the right time to stop or continue; they are able to judge their own moments of personal readiness, for example, looking between their legs and performing all sorts of tumbling activities before embarking on a forward somersault. David, aged four, is seen in Photograph 45 trying out what it is like to be nearly upside down. He has three points of contact with the floor – the head and two hands. Perhaps he wants to do a forward roll. Or he may not know what will happen next and the result will come as a surprise. The surprise element is a common one with young children and is usually followed in one of two ways; either with delight, in which case the feat is attempted again this time anticipating the outcome, or the shock is too great and the activity is hurriedly left to return to at another time.

Photograph 45   Three points of balance

Landscaping, featuring banks, slopes, hills, trees, gullies, stepping stones and river banks provides a more extensive range of opportunities for acrobatic and athletic activities than can be experienced at home. 'Significant other people' as described by Bruce (1997) feature prominently here, as in the other areas of activity; a hand to steady legs in first attempts to balance upside down, to help the head tuck in as a forward roll is begun, to hold the stick to be jumped over are important contributors to the learning experience.

Water play and beyond

Agility in the water is equally valued as part of early childhood provision. The enjoyment of bath times, garden paddling pools and visits to the children's pools at the local baths all combine to make children water-confident and secure. Moving into, through, under and on top of water are excellent fore-runners of water skills, life skills which for obvious reasons should be intro-duced as early as possible.

Photograph 46   Zach loves his bath and enjoys splashing

Learning of many kinds takes place during these early water activities and this is particularly so where there are toys, floats and other equipment to hand. I am reminded of the play of two toddlers aged about two years who were sitting in the water on the steps of a pool. One girl discovered a plastic jug floating on the surface which she filled with water and gently poured over the head of the other. While doing so she talked about washing her friend's hair and her friend played her part by bending her head forward and closing her eyes. Then, as if she had just remembered that there was another aspect of hair-washing, 'the hairdresser' put just a little water into the jug this time and applied it as a shampoo rather than a rinse, rubbing it into the scalp. Who could have antic-ipated that these domestic activities would have come about through the jux-taposition of water, jug and friend? Who could have anticipated that by carrying out the actions of washing the hair the toddler 'became' the mother or the hairdresser, that her initial actions led to characterisation?

Once children become self-reliant in local pools, swimming baths and water parks the time is probably ripe for encouraging activities of keeping afloat and propulsion through the water – swimming! It is important that the fun element is kept in the foreground of this next developmental phase and that family and friends remain actively involved in the learning process, continuing to provide opportunities and security. For example, when a mother swims carrying a child on her back all sorts of learning take place in this shared activity where schemas are introduced, shared or re-enforced. Such learning includes:

• feeling the rhythm of the activity involving effort and recovery
• breathing in and out
• the horizontal trajectory focus of the travelling – across the pool
• the amount of space covered – a little or a long way
• the sense of balancing on a moving object.

As they make 'water journeys' like these, young children often wave to people standing on the side as they pass to draw attention to what is taking place. As confidence grows children become more active in rides of this sort. They may imitate the arm movements of the carrier, not necessarily matching them in timing but nevertheless getting the feel of the activity of swimming. As they progress a time comes when children are ready to swim a few strokes on their own. Frequently this is towards an adult waiting with outstretched arms ready to receive and praise or, in sensing a difficulty, prepared to move forward and retrieve. Once well versed in this activity it may be time to increase the distance being covered or suggest that the rail at the side of the pool replaces the adult as the goal.

At the first attempts to swim, at whatever age they appear, it is important to encourage the wholeness of whatever 'stroke' the child is attempting rather than concentrating on separate operations such as arms, legs or body action. Much later specific skills assume importance and become a matter for 'coaching'. Magill writes interestingly about practising skills as either wholes or in parts and, although his work does not encompass learning in the ways it is approached in early childhood education, the following extract is extremely helpful in this particular context. He points out:

An argument in favor of practicing a skill as a whole is that this experience would help a learner get a better feel for the flow and timing of all the component movements of the skill.   (Magill 1998: 252)

In all these examples of water-sited activity, progression from the zone of proximal development to potential development can clearly be seen to operate. Of course, advancement is not a straightforward, linear affair and, as Nutbrown (1994: 24) reminds us:

> *It may be helpful to think of the notion of 'schemas revisited', where children build up their knowledge through their absorption in particular schemas and, later, with more maturity of action, language and thought return to explore a schema further.*

Where games begin

Here the important aim is to provide an environment *to develop children's dexterity and, primarily, their attempts to make objects move or to deal with those already moving.* Wetton (1988: 111) calls these 'manipulative skills'. Development is sometimes seen to be less marked than in the other areas of movement activity not least because it involves elements of unpredictability and change. Consequently much current literature tends to focus on developments that occur at five years and beyond. An exception is the Physical Development section in the *Curriculum Guidance for the Foundation Stage* where some examples of what children can do are identified and related to the responsibilities of practitioners (QCA 2000: 100–5). However, the curriculum guide is for children aged three through to the end of the reception year and, as suggested in the opening text, 'children will have already learnt a great deal by the time they are three years old' (ibid.: 6). In the case of manipulative play, the basis is clearly observable from a very early age. Some of the features that characterise the prowess of our top footballers, cricketers and basketball players can be seen in the movement of quite young babies. Reaching, grasping, releasing, focusing, tracking, hitting, pushing and pulling are only a few of these. As well as actions, play strategies are also in evidence as babies involve themselves in solo games such as grasping a toy and dropping it onto the floor. While babies are absorbed in their own solo games with early self-made rules, parents are often eager to engage in games for two. This might involve the baby reaching out and taking something from an adult which is then put into the mouth.

As indicated earlier, making objects move is a complex operation where attention has to be given to both the body and the object being rolled, thrown, caught, struck or propelled in some other way. Bouncing a ball, which when mastered seems such a simple activity, is an example of a constantly changing operation often presenting four- and five-year-olds with difficulties in perception and hand-eye co-ordination. It is a considerable challenge to combine agility, athletic prowess and manipulative skill in activities of this kind. The complexity of such operations makes it clear why young children have to concentrate so intently, why there is such a constant need to practise and why there is such a diversity of attainment in this area of movement. Photograph 47 shows how far Richard, who is six, has come in catching a ball. He is focusing well and his arms and hands are ready to receive it. Soon he will learn to step towards it so that he is in the right place. As he gains confidence from increased experience and success, the bound flow restriction that currently characterises his stance will lessen, although he will need to keep hold of some of this in order to be precise and efficient.

Photograph 47   Early attempts at catching

In providing for experience in games-oriented activities, a range of types of equipment, as well as a variety of shapes, sizes and colour, are important. Very young children need objects that are soft and malleable to grasp in initial attempts to throw and catch while striking surfaces need to be wide. The introduction of harder materials and reduction in size implies greater expertise on the part of the handler. So, too, does the manipulation of two pieces of apparatus, for example, a bat and a ball.

Shall we dance?

Dance is arguably the least difficult area of provision to make at home. Yet, perhaps because it seems less tangible than its counterparts, it is often the area least well catered for. In the absence of permanent external structures such as agility apparatus, bats and balls to occupy limbs or to direct focus, dance-like activity is most often only fleetingly glimpsed and not always registered. While welcoming such transient moments of predominantly spontaneous activity, dance, like all other types of movement, needs to be woven into the daily routine. Above all children need space to dance which may entail pushing furniture to the walls, opening up communicating rooms or finding a quiet corner of the garden. There are lots of resources which can be used in encouraging children to dance and these are identified in Chapter 7. The part played by brothers, sisters, parents and friends cannot be underestimated. Taking part alongside others is something young children enjoy and to be a partner who is held in the arms of an adult and 'danced' is a particular joy as is dancing with them.

Moving away from home: provision for the youngest children

At home both the nature and extent of movement provision relate to personal decisions by parents and availability of space. It varies within and between home units, in regularity and content. From the home base, transitions into a wider environment are incorporated dependent upon personal circumstances and child rearing philosophies. The result is that quite young children will experience parent and toddler groups or spend time with a child minder, whether this is a professional, a neighbour or a member of the family, before going on to a part- or full-time early childhood setting.

Photograph 48   Harriet and her mother dance together

Since the introduction of *Curriculum Guidance for the Foundation Stage* in 2000 there has been a change in attitude and practice for children aged from three to the end of the reception year. Rather than provision reflecting the value systems of isolated establishments, the current curriculum guidelines go much further than previous common consensus that children less than five years of age need to engage in physical activity. While it seems similar to how it takes place in the home, the way in which movement is featured in early childhood settings is different in kind. It looks at effective learning and links it with the role of the practitioner who is considered an important constituent in the planning and implementation process. In terms of resources, provision may also be similar to that of the best home settings but in most cases there will be a greater variety and used in the company of children engaged in similar developmental sequencing. The design of agility structures is likely to be more informed and, at its best, provides a common resource, both indoors and out. Children of this age need both stable and mobile equipment which use the large muscle groups; barrels and tyres they can crawl through, trucks and trolleys and a variety of wheeled toys they can push, pull and pedal.

Photograph 49   Sorting out energy, load and number

For the three children in Photograph 49 transport play was a rich learning situation. Increasing passengers from one to two produced some initial difficulty for the 'driver' in making a start and in keeping going. *'It won't go'* she said. The ensuing conversation between the children about the reasons for this increased difficulty involved talking about:

- energy on the part of the 'driver', who realised that she had to pedal much harder
- weight, because it was more heavily loaded
- numbers because there were two passengers instead of one.

Although not discussed by the children it was interesting to note that steering was also affected. No longer was 'cornering' included in the journeys they made, which now consisted of straight pathways taken at a slow pace. Ideally, these children will be encouraged to take part in similar situations in which they can compare weight, number and energy output, and come to further conclusions based on their own experiential observations. An important role of early childhood educators is to make the most of what each and every child has to offer when they join the Foundation Stage setting. One such role, identified by Athey and which continues as a major one through-out the whole of primary education, is to:

> *feed spontaneous structures with content not necessarily found at home, street or playground. In other words, worthwhile curriculum content can be offered that, if received, will extend cognitive structures educationally.* (Athey 1990: 41)

Given an overall acceptance that movement provision is an important constituent of early childhood, its nature and content relate to a variety of care and education issues in evidence at a time when rapid physical and intellectual development characterise the life of the children who attend.

Provision in primary schools

One of the major differences for the children entering mainstream education is in the structure of the day. Particular areas of learning have their set place and allotted time span within a nationally agreed curriculum at Key Stages 1 and 2. Core subjects of English, Mathematics and Science are supported by nine subjects, one of which is Physical Education which includes Dance. Although it is suggested that schools may choose how they organise their curriculum to include programmes of study for each of the designated subjects, evidence shows that the majority of time is given to the core subjects. It is interesting to observe that at the beginning of the *Handbook for Primary Teachers in England* there is a special note about Physical Education which reads:

> *The Government believes that two hours of physical activity a week, including the National Curriculum for physical education and extra curricular activities, should be an aspiration for all schools. This applies through all key stages.*
> (DfEE and QCA 1999: 16)

In essence primary school children should be able to participate in any of the seven separate areas of the movement curriculum (athletics, dance, games, gymnastics, outdoor and adventurous activities, and swimming) all of which, as we have seen, have their roots in the movement activities of early child-hood. It is encouraging for early childhood educators to know that, if children have been given appropriate provision, support and guidance in early movement activities at home and in early childhood settings, they should be

well prepared for the transition into primary education. However, it is difficult to reconcile what teachers know their young pupils need with the time
allowance given. Unofficial reports show that, although there are some
schools that somehow make the time, on the whole the broad spread of
physical education subjects remain underutilised.

Amidst all the provision essential for the education and care of young children the most important resource continues to be the adults who:

- are professionally educated in matters of child development
- promote and organise a relevant range of learning experiences
- select appropriate equipment and materials
- are on hand throughout the day to give increased meaning to activities
  undertaken
- assess, monitor and record the children's learning
- reflect upon their own practice to inform future decision making and
  change.

According to Ball (1994: 56) their calibre and training are key determinants
of high-quality provision. This view is supported by Nutbrown (1994: 155)
who, in making a case that young children should be respected as capable
thinkers and learners, goes on to say that such respect should be acknowledged by:

> ensuring that the adults who work with young children are well trained, well
> qualified, experienced to manage the diversity of the task and respected
> members of a professional group who receive due reward and recognition for
> their work.

Learning situations: a flexible guide

Although ways in which learning and teaching strategies take place are different in the home, early years, infant and junior school settings, there are
certain phases of experience common to all of these. These four phases can
usefully serve as guidelines for all types of activity sessions and by children
of all ages provided they are used flexibly and relevantly:

- free exploration
- guided exploration
- consolidation
- extension.

Free exploration

Free exploration means exactly what it says, referring to children's untutored response to any movement-related situation in which they find themselves – in a cot, beside a stream, on a grassy slope or in a highly organised gymnastics or dance lesson. Free exploration allows children to move in any way they wish; to try out activities and ideas. It describes an open-ended, non-interventionist learning situation, and represents one end of a continuum which has, at its other end, direct and detailed teaching of set skills. It occurs at times when, activated only by personal wishes and within safety limits provided by those responsible, children investigate the static, mobile and artistic environment in which they find themselves. The general view of the physical educationalists of the 1970s was that exploration was an early discrete phase followed by more advanced strategies such as skill acquisition and problem-solving. The implication of this view was interpreted by some to mean that problems are not solved, skill is not acquired through exploration and people cease to explore after they are young. In fact, free exploration applies to all stages of movement education and recreative pursuits and is a serious and significant activity.

Movement schemas and free exploration

The wide-ranging set of movement possibilities seen in terms of the body, space, dynamics and relationships, as set out in Chapter 1, could be relevantly re-classified as a repertoire of 'schemas'. Children arriving at nursery school have at their disposal a number of actions such as running, jumping, balancing, gesturing, twirling and climbing, and know about such things as being high up and low down, stretched out and curled up, and moving slowly and quickly. Free exploration of a new environment allows these bodily, dynamic and spatial schemas to be used to the full. Athey (1990: 37) suggests, 'Experience is [thus] assimilated to cognitive structures and this is how knowledge is acquired'. The intensity with which children use a currently compelling schema cannot be mistaken. Using their vertical schemas, they repeatedly climb up and down the scrambling net, twirl round and round illustrating interest in the spatial concept of circularity and, incorporating the use of dynamic schemas, pedal a tricycle energetically along paths. A similar intensity may be seen in the 'intertwining' activities of eight-year-olds as they try out their bodily mobility on the agility frame or dribble a ball up and down the football pitch.

It is important that schemas are recognised in movement as well as in other aspects of children's learning and this is particularly true in terms of dynamics. Bruce (1997: 70) draws our attention to the fact that 'early childhood settings, schools and parents tend to encourage the configurative aspects of schemas more than the dynamic aspects'.

Extending schemas

Sometimes children's schemas are 'opened out' a little and they become more generalised. For example, there will be a time when four-year-olds well experienced in balancing along the library wall, the high kerbstone outside the school or in other familiar locations may be ready to seize upon other opportunities to balance. This could occur in the park with the discovery of two parallel poles with a space in between as part of the agility apparatus in the children's playground. Faced with the prospect of balancing in this new situation children may be able to use their current action schema of balancing or, alternatively, may have to modify it in order to accommodate the unfamiliar structure. Modifying or accommodating behaviour of this kind was observed in the attempts of a seven-year-old girl, Tanya, who, adept at climbing fixed vertical ladders, met a rope ladder for the first time. Clearly, she was not prepared for several of the differences which she encountered:

- the mobile, swinging nature of the rope ladder
- its fixture at one end only
- the rope which replaced wood.

Equally clear, however, was that, despite these significant differences, some features of the rope ladder *were* familiar to her. The horizontal rungs and the verticality of the ladder were the very things which, in the first instance, probably suggested to her that here was a place where she could fulfil her love of climbing. Only after a great deal of practice did she emerge equipped with an extended set of climbing-related schemas – and with increased self-confidence.

Schemas become more co-ordinated

In arguing for periods of free exploration for learners of all ages, it is important to stress that there should be some element present which makes the situation different for young children at home and in early childhood settings from those attending infant and junior schools. As the process of assimilation continues through life the difference must necessarily lie within the schemas themselves. Like all schemas, movement schemas gradually become more co-ordinated and include a host of complicated ideas. At the simplest level might be the attempts of a five-year-old to swing on a rope while the agile way in which most eight-year-olds can use one or two ropes to swing and climb illustrates a more advanced level. At the far end of the spectrum is the trapeze artist who can swing using a variety of body parts for support and execute a series of dynamically compelling stunts in the air. At the highest level of functioning we find choreographers composing from armchairs and Olympic coaches making up routines for the parallel bars far from the sports hall. Action has truly become internalised thought.

Guided exploration

Although through provision and comment there is a small element of in-built guidance in free exploration, its presence in guided exploration is more specific in terms of facilitating, shaping and influencing movement outcomes. Experiences which are adult led refer to the channelling of movement responses through opportunities, suggestions, tasks and challenges set by parents, teachers and others involved. Used appropriately it is a phase of learning which, through degrees of limitation, brings about:

- greater versatility
- increasing skilfulness
- clarity of intent and outcome.

Adult-encouraged experience varies greatly according to the context in which it is used. Usually the younger or more inexperienced the child, the wider and more generalised the movement challenge. It is relatively easy to find appropriate challenges for individual children as they move at home or in early childhood settings and to pick up on what they have been recently doing. For example, suitable suggestions might be 'to find places to jump from the frame', to 'try out the things you were doing on the mat' or 'to dance to a favourite piece of music'. Sometimes, however, parents and teachers have to relate to a small group of children who are sharing space or equipment, in which case, the suggestions made have to be general enough for each child to take up. Limitation of any kind demands some degree of accommodation on the part of individuals and the more specific and demanding the task the less likely everyone in the group or class will be able to comply. Challenges can be simple or complex and narrow or wide in design according to the amount of individual response envisaged. In the next chapter, suggestions for challenging children's movement invention and skill at varying stages of development will be listed but, at this point, it might be helpful to think of individuals or groups of children who would be able to cope with the following suggestions. To have particular children in mind, as these are read, helps to fit challenges to landmarks of learning:

- Make your hands and feet dance to the music.
- Stretch your body as much as you can while you move on the apparatus.
- Practise bouncing your ball at different heights as you run with it.
- Move on your hands and feet on the agility frame and travel in one direction only.
- Make up a dance which has three sections and end small and close to the ground.

As children's expertise grows and their movement schemas become increasingly complex and co-ordinated, so set patterns of movement begin to play a part in lessons as well as in outside clubs and organisations. Ballet and contemporary dance classes, skiing holidays, swimming, rambling and games clubs are just a few of the out-of-school activities which begin to command interest at this point.

Consolidation

Children need time to consolidate and become secure in their recently acquired skills. As well as carrying out their activities in familiar contexts they need to reinforce them in situations of similar difficulty. There is sometimes a tendency or temptation to build one layer of skilful or inventive activity on top of another – a hierarchically structured pattern of learning – which often results in stress as increasingly difficult challenges are not able to be met. It is hard for adults not to encourage so-called advancement because they know only too well what can come next. It is not unknown for some primary school children (perhaps, in part, expressing the anxiety of parents) to want to go on to the next, more complex book – because to do so implies progress and 'keeping up' – rather than to enjoy other books of a comparable standard and thus come to love the activity and reward of reading for pleasure and reading with ease. Such lateral experience, or sideways extension, essential to good practice in literacy, is equally important in movement education. It is important because, in this way, children are given opportunities to use their new movement knowledge and understanding, be it in dance, games or gymnastics, in a variety of situations and, not least, because it gives the current state of children's experience, the here and now, as much value as any anticipated, future goal. Margaret Donaldson (1978: 32) warned about the danger of 'acquiring language rather than learning to speak'. In similar vein, Keith Swanwick (1982: 9), referring specifically to arts education, argues that:

> *Education is surely more than having 'experiences' or acquiring a repertoire of skills and facts. It has to do with developing understanding, insightfulness; qualities of mind.*

Although Swanwick's words refer to arts education, they can be applied equally well to the whole of movement education. His message, and that of Donaldson, signify that the acquisition of the language of movement is not necessarily synonymous with learning to move.

In making a case for the inclusion of lateral experiences at each stage of development we should remember that children sometimes need to be encouraged to part company with movement activities with which they appear to be stuck and which have become rather meaningless. This may be a particular activity like rolling down the bank, a special dance or a favourite ball game. In all such situations adults will need to find ways for the children to 'move on', ways which, while respecting the familiar, will incorporate manageable units of unfamiliarity and thus ensure progression.

Extension

This refers to a phase of activity where the aim is for children to enlarge and combine their movement schemas and thus become more versatile, skilful and 'personalised' in what they do. Children will perceive for themselves ways in which their activities can be extended. Readers will perhaps remember times from their own childhood when they went to bed hardly bearing to leave their current 'craze' and already thinking about what they were going to do with it the next day. However, in addition to free extension of this self-imposed sort, challenges set specifically for the children, and which are adult led, play an increasingly important role in early childhood education, coming fully to fruition in the infant and junior school when adults become re-cast as teachers. Once again the complexity of demands needs to coincide with the current sequence of functioning reached by individuals and groups of children. This implies that those involved in presenting those challenges need to be able to match them accurately.

Matching

Children are the best 'matchers' in the world. They not only make good judges of what to do next but also of when to do it. Their ability here has some connection with the notion of 'seriated difficulty', which we looked at in detail earlier, although versatility also plays an important part. Evidence of 'self-match' is plentiful as children volunteer what they are 'going to do next' or seek to show 'what they have just done'. Talking and assessing together at this juncture is an important part of learning and helps to consolidate what has taken place.

It is hard for teachers and parents to be as expert as their children in shaping progressive challenges which provide just the right amount of disturbance to their equilibrium, especially when dealing with groups or whole classes rather than individuals. But it is worthwhile persevering. The key to satisfactory matching lies in finding challenges which the children can manage. This means estimating where they are functioning at any given time and then finding just the right potential extension for them to attempt. The lack of research and consequent dearth of sufficiently specific guidelines relating to the pitching of appropriate challenges is a severe disadvantage in movement education. Athey (1990: 16) suggests that the greatest progress has been made in 'matching' what children can do with what children are offered in mathematics, science and language. On the other hand, there is an abundance of first-hand evidence of children's own do-it-yourself movement activity to guide us. The degree of struggle between what children can do and the demands of the next stage of achievement equates to the size of the gap between the two. The triumph of the 'I've done it' variety is seen in contrast to the anxiety and despondency shown when the discrepancy was too great, resulting in cries of 'I can't do it' or 'I give up'.

Even within these two extremes care must be taken to make sure we have 'gauged it right'. For example, in the first instance, the ability to solve the problem could be too immediate and effortless, demanding too small a leap while, in the second case, some additional help in the initial stages might make all the necessary difference to eventual success. Excessive praise might be as inappropriate a response in one situation as supporting the child's wish to give up in the other. As Roberts (2002: 55) points out:

> *It really matters that we only give praise where it's due, and don't fall into the habit of praising on all occasions, 'to be on the safe side'. In fact the safe side is just what it is not, as children who are praised indiscriminately soon come to suspect that all praise is meaningless.*

Practice

Built into the children's ability to match up to movement challenges is the notion of practice which goes hand in hand with their current level of under-standing and interest. Brearley (1969: 180) differentiates between the kind of practising which takes place in relation to a set challenge and the passionate practising seen when young children use the apparatus at the start of a lesson. If a challenge is the children's own then so is their inner motivation and drive; through their practising they will be able to judge their own suc-cess or failure, to reach or fall short of their own inner models. At any time in the process they can change their model in response to how they view suc-cess or failure. For example, a seven-year-old may set himself the challenge of vaulting over an agility box but, having tried this once or twice, without apparent success, he may change to jumping onto the box, travelling along it and jumping off the other end – perhaps convincing himself that this was what was intended right from the start! A four-year-old, hesitating at the opening of the tunnel, may decide to run to the other end and look into it from there instead of making the expected journey through.

   However, this does not necessarily mean that attempts to carry out the original activity cease. Or that children do not accept practice in relation to challenges other than the ones they set themselves. Practice is associated with all sorts of different learning situations and the main criterion is that it is personally meaningful and effective.

Half an hour with Lucy: an assessment of action schemas

This chapter is brought to an end with comments on a thirty-minute play period which Lucy, aged three ('four next Thursday'), shared with her mother. Lucy's play is seen in the context of a movement-based environment, the ways in which young children develop for themselves a skilled and versatile activity life, and how they interact with people. Learning and teaching phases of free and guided exploration, consolidation and extension are looked at in the ways they relate to Lucy's activities. The role of Lucy's mother as she participates, looks and listens, sets the scene for the next chapter when the support, enrichment and extension of early movement activities are discussed.

On this occasion, Lucy's play environment consisted of a large, grassed area which sloped down to a straight, concrete path. Two sets of stone steps, each with a railing, plus two outsize rubber balls completed the scene. Generally, the level of movement activity during the thirty-minute period was high. Lucy's action schemas included walking, running, balancing, jumping, galloping and turning. Although she changed freely from one to another throughout the afternoon, two schemas appeared to be particularly actively explored.

Jumping

Lucy found all sorts of places to jump: she leapt onto the large rubber balls, into her mother's arms and across the grass. At one point, using the path as a track, she made up a variety of jumping patterns, jumping from two feet to two feet, from one foot to the other and from one foot to the same foot. From this personal collection Lucy persevered with her two-to-two jump, eventually 'accommodating' this to one of the two flights of steps. Starting at the fifth stair, she jumped down the steps one at a time towards her mother who waited at the bottom ready to give her a high lift into the air to mark the end of the sequence (Photograph 50). Lucy did this several times and it is interesting to note that, unlike Alexandra, tipping herself off the steps into her father's arms, Lucy was pushing off and achieving a 'real' jump. This was the first time Lucy had done this activity.

Turning

Turning was the second of Lucy's action schemas which featured significantly in her play as she tumbled, half rolled, and turned round and round. She also experienced the sensation of turning in circles as her mother swung her round in a horizontal plane, parallel to the ground. Later, when Lucy was once again tumbling and turning on the grass, her mother asked 'Can you do this?' and quickly went into a cartwheel. Although the complexity of hand–foot co-ordination and the proximity of limbs for the purposes of weight-bearing were not within Lucy's comprehension, she immediately

Photograph 50   Pushing off and coming down

Photograph 51 Turning and jumping: a co-ordinated schema

absorbed the circularity of the movement and managed a 'twisty turn'. This was another 'first' to add to her personal movement repertoire, one which readily became one of her favourites to which she returned time and time again, and one which developed in understanding and skill throughout the afternoon. Later still, on returning to the path on which she originally tried out her jumping game, Lucy put together her two most practised schemas – jumping and turning. Running along the path she took off and turned in the air. She was airborne for only a moment and rose only a few inches from the ground but nevertheless, as can be seen in Photograph 51, it was indeed a turning jump. And a wonderful accomplishment.

A new shape

One further discovery Lucy made during this intensive period of play was a new shape – a star shape where she became wide and stretched – and which she can be seen sharing with her mother in Photograph 4 (in Chapter 1). Her pleasure in this newly found activity was obvious and throughout the afternoon, and seemingly without any reason, she would take it up time and time again.

Assessing Lucy's play

Lucy was involved in all four learning situations set out earlier on in this chapter. Much of her initial and intermittent activity was exploratory where she made her own responses to the steps, railings and grassy slopes of her immediate environment as well as to the acrobatic and athletic potential of her long and lean body. From time to time her mother led her into the second phase of learning by initiating activity through verbal suggestions or via her own activity. Where these were taken up the ideas were appropriately pursued, but when Lucy showed either disinterest or dislike the idea was immediately abandoned. In these instances, Lucy usually took herself away for a short time and did something familiar, and loved, indicating that the distance between what she could do and what she was asked to do was too great. She could not accommodate to the new challenge. Lucy's involvement in the third phase of consolidation was seen when she tried out her separate jumping and turning in a variety of different, but similarly demanding, situations before going on to extend them. Eventually, her most complex co-ordination of the afternoon emerged when her action schema of turning was joined with her action schema of jumping to produce a turn in the air.

The way in which Lucy's mother was able to participate actively in Lucy's play was clearly a bonus in her learning experience. The dynamic, spatial images which she shared with her daughter through her bodily activity, and the excitement and pleasure she communicated on her own and Lucy's account, helped to make the experience an inviting and reassuring one. The words which Lucy's mother used to identify, describe and expand her movements, and the questions she asked, demanding both movement and verbal answers, also helped Lucy in her 'moving and knowing'. Whitehead (1990: 81) writes of the importance of children's language development in this way:

> *A central concern of teachers should be to find ways of unlocking children's linguistic potential: stimulating a wider extension of active vocabulary resources and supporting more complex language performance.*

In addition to practising current activities, and finding new ones, Lucy liked to recall earlier experiences. One of these was her 'floor dance' which she performed with the path as her stage and at the end of which she gave a deep bow. There could be several reasons why this particular dance activity might have re-emerged as it did. Lucy's mother is involved in dance education and, therefore, dance is a familiar activity. But, over and above that, Lucy was full of the fact that she was being taken to see *Coppelia* as a birthday treat. She could sing some of the music and remembered the story as it had been read to her a year or so previously.

Lucy's repetition and co-ordination of movement schemas throughout this period of activity has provided a fascinating study. It would be interesting now to continue these observations and record the next stage of development in Lucy's movement and dance play.

Summary

The importance of the schema to the early childhood educator is that it provides a mechanism for analysing 'where the learner is' and helps predict analogous situations which will be of interest to the child (Bruce 1997: 73).

5

Supporting, extending and enriching movement

We speak of starting with a child 'where he is', which in one sense is not to assert an educational desideratum but an inescapable fact; there is no other place the child can start from. There are only other places the educator can start from.   (Bissex 1980: 111)

Selecting appropriate learning phases

In the previous chapter the phases of *free and guided exploration, consolidation and extension* were selected because they relate comfortably to movement education as a specific area of learning and they can be used flexibly in a variety of movement contexts from the earliest years at home through to lessons at Key Stages 1 and 2. Knowing what each phase represents, parents, family, friends, and early childhood professionals can decide which ones are best suited to their children's current learning interests. At home, where one-to-one relationships often prevail, the sequence of phases will relate in the main to activities initiated by the children themselves. As children widen their experience outside the home a variety of increasingly organised contexts, suggestions and challenges are likely to become more small-group and class oriented.

The following guidelines, governing the selection of learning phases, are thought to be appropriate for a variety of situations in which 'assisted movement learning' takes place. They can be used by adults who engage in the early movement play of their children, by early childhood educators and childminders who cater for individuals and small groups, and by class teachers in the preparation and translation into more structured lessons. In all these settings it is important to keep the following guidelines in mind.

- All phases are important in the movement development of children up to eight years.

- There is no hierarchical ordering of phases.
- Not every movement session/lesson has to start with free exploration.
- There is not a special phase.
- Phases may be taken out of order and occur more than once.
- Phases may take up different lengths of time.
- Not all phases have to happen in one movement session/lesson.
- Phases may be combined.

The object now is to look at how phases may be used within several different learning/teaching situations and to consider ways in which some of the theoretical ideas introduced earlier tie up with the movement classification looked at in Chapter 1.

A flexible approach

The general format for informal activity sessions at one end of the birth to eight-year age range and more structured lessons at the other has common threads, although the nature of the challenges set, the use of teaching devices and the child expectations are very different. There is nothing sacrosanct about every detail of content; some ideas are interchangeable although the treatment of them may differ. For example, the dance theme of fireworks as set out in Chapter 8 may be used in a different way with younger or older age groups. Similarly, the 'dance play' session, pitched at the level of three- and four-year-olds, which also appears in Chapter 8, may be reshaped and extended in a variety of ways for children in infant and junior schools. It is the relationship of the various elements, along with the measure for potential development, which defines suitability in each case.

All spontaneous and structured activity sessions along the lines of those which follow contain free exploration and also what might be termed guided contributions. These include the roles which parents, early years practitioners and teachers play, teaching styles and ways which enable maximum learning to take place. They are used here as structuring agents; they identify ways in which the most can be made of periods of children's activity whenever and wherever that activity takes place. It might be argued that common guidelines bring about inflexibility and closed opportunities, but the opposite is true. Because the flexible use of phases of learning implies knowledge of child development and movement principles, both input and outcomes can be varied and relevant. Important elements in the examples given are:

- setting the scene
- observing the outcome
- giving feedback
- engaging in dialogue.

Making suggestions and setting challenges

Sometimes adults need to find ways to set children off; to stimulate, to lead, to interest, to involve them. This can be through the kinds of material provision talked about earlier. It may also come about through talking with the children about what they are in the process of doing or through sharing suggestions as to what they might do next. As cognitive, emotional and physical development advance the 'take it or leave it' type of suggestion, frequently used with young children who are working individually, is extended by teacher-guided challenges which can be appropriately answered by all the children in a small group or class. Relevant, open-ended challenges encourage appropriate movement responses and, therefore, hold no danger of children being unable to respond. They are used to encourage exploration and improvisation, to allow time for children to engage in and consolidate previous learning, and to open up areas of potential achievement. In the *Curriculum Guidance for the Foundation Stage* one of the principles refers to opportunities for children to engage in activities planned by adults and also those that they plan themselves (QCA 2000: 11).

In writing about open-ended versus closed structures, Bruce (1991: 89) draws attention to Jack, aged four years, who was asked to make a fish using a template and prescribed materials – milk bottle tops for scales and tissue paper for the tail. Personal decisions in Jack's fish activity were minimal and, in comparison, adult expectations of what the end product should look like were high. The movement equivalent of such an experience could be found in precisely fashioned skill sequences which simply do not enter into the early years of learning. As Wetton (1988: Introduction) reminds us, 'The younger the child, the more the teacher, nursery nurse or auxiliary will need to concentrate on personalising and individualising the child's experiences'.

At other times, rather than responding to wide-view suggestions introduced by adults, interest is triggered by seeing other people, either children or adults, engaged in a particular form of movement. 'Children are affected by the context in which learning takes place, the people involved in it, and the values and beliefs which are embedded in it' (DES, 1990: 67–8).

Observation

A central characteristic which comes to the fore, when considering children's learning in movement, is the adult's ability to observe quickly and accurately. Swift and informed observation means that assessment can be immediate, and feedback equally so. Without the help that arises from good observation techniques children can be 'strangle-held' in an activity for longer than is necessary or fulfilling. Indicating the importance of observation in short-term planning for young children Fisher (1996: 143) writes:

> *Through observation in action, carrying out open-ended tasks which allow them to explore and investigate, teachers can gain information about children's knowledge and understanding as well as their skills and strategies. All of this information is necessary if teachers are to plan a curriculum which has relevance and purpose for each child.*

For example, a girl near to performing a backward somersault over a pole may just need to know that she should let her head go back with the rest of her upper body as she brings her legs up to the pole. To explain that she is nearly there but not quite making it because her head is restricting the circular passage of movement, and to receive instantaneous encouragement and help to put the words into practice, may mean that she meets with success sooner than later. Such advice, support and encouragement, resulting from skilled observation is in tune with the 'potential' level of development, suggested by Vygotsky and referred to earlier.

Observation also provides material for long-term movement assessment and evaluation on which records and profiles are based. An interesting view of the importance of observation in children's play is presented by Hurst (1994: 173) who writes of the challenge for early childhood educators to learn from observation and identifies purposes and procedures in the learning/teaching situation. Everyone involved in education acknowledges the importance of observation. The many tasks and monitoring demands attributed to teachers could not be carried out without observational references. However, its practice within movement, which is transitory in nature, brings with it a particular set of problems that needs to be separately addressed. The examples of record-keeping based on movement observations given throughout this book refer to specific situations, but there is also a general need for both early childhood and movement practitioners and theorists to examine the nature of this important aspect of assessing, recording and monitoring movement, at greater depth, in more detail and over time.

Knowing *what to assess* in terms of activities, processes or products is as important as knowing *how to assess* in terms of strategies and pedagogy. Linfield and Warwick (1996: 84) explain that:

> *Having a grasp of the development of conceptual and procedural understanding allows the educator to plan purposefully, and to use observation as a genuine assessment tool.*

Nutbrown (1994: 39) ascertains that prolonged time spans play an important part in the observational process and advocates that:

> *One of the clearest ways to understand progression in children's learning is to look at individuals over a period of time, observing their schematic interests, seeing how these relate to the development of their behaviour, their speech and their thinking.*

Clearly, movement can take its place alongside other areas of learning, sharing the common core to which Hurst refers while identifying its own 'peculiarities'.

Looking and talking together

Whatever their age, wherever they may be, whatever they are doing, talking to children about their movement is a major part of the learning situation. It provides the means whereby achievement and understanding can be assessed and it also features prominently in the recording process. The questions adults and children ask, as well as help and guidance given to individuals and like-minded groups as they work, are of the utmost importance. Such inter-conversational interludes are highly valued by children and adults alike, with the time spent on talking together increasing in length and complexity as children's concentration spans extend. Another significant factor influencing the manner in which children and adults look and talk together is in relation to 'whose movement it is'. With very young children their concentration, and their conversation, is predictably on 'me and my movement'. It may be some time before the movement of others is of lasting interest. The dialogue between children also plays an important part in their learning bringing with it an affinity and reciprocity different in kind from the adult–child relation-ship. This view supports the research carried out by Mosston and Ashworth whose spectrum of teaching styles although not oriented to early childhood experiences in movement, is nevertheless pertinent here. In setting the scene for new roles and new relationships they maintain that the teacher accepts the socialising process between observer and doer as a desirable goal in education (Mosston and Ashworth 1994: 67). The implementation of the reciprocal teaching style where the teacher 'is able to shift the power of giving feedback to the learner' is particularly relevant to the seven- and eight-year-olds participating in more structured situations. However, whether the occasion is spontaneous or structured it follows that encouraging children to talk with each other about what is happening, and to exchange views, is educationally sound.

We can see from the wide range of questions asked of the children in the following two sample activity sessions that the notion of movement-matching operates similarly in terms of language. Questions have to be of the right sort for the children to be able to think about and answer in an appropriate manner. With the youngest children, questions need to be asso-ciated in some way to the 'here and now' of their activity, to what is within their immediate grasp and of a 'matter of fact' variety. Questions of the 'I wonder if' and 'supposing' type guard against the closed, predictable nature of answers. Advice given in the *Curriculum Guidance for the Foundation Stage* emphasises that using conversations and carefully framed questions is crucial in developing children's knowledge, and here open-endedness is clearly stated:

Conversations, open-ended questions and thinking out loud are important tools in developing vocabulary and challenging thinking. Encouraging children to reflect on and tell others what they have been doing ... helps them to give voice to what they know and to practise thinking and new vocabulary.

(QCA 2000: 23)

Later on, children are able to surmise a little, to allow those 'ifs' and 'buts' into their descriptions and conversations and are able to deviate from the immediate situation. Meadows and Cashdan (1988: 59) point out that:

whenever we ask a question we are making a 'demand' on that child ... The teacher who is aware of the range of possible levels of demand is in a good position to vary questions appropriately, striking the best balance between extending the child and consolidating their existing knowledge.

One of the overriding values of language exchange within the movement session is the clarification and articulation of the skills, versatility and artistry the children are achieving: to describe both the process – what is taking place – and the end product, if there is one.

The younger children

In the case of the two- and three-year-olds the major part of movement activity times will be started spontaneously by the children themselves or in response to the sort of provision made for them. At other times, joining in with parents or older brothers' and sisters' activities brings about enhanced understanding as well as a strong sense of camaraderie. Times such as these prove to be great favourites with the children as long as the main emphasis is on the 'doing', or perhaps what might be more appropriately called 'me doing'. As we saw with Lucy's play session in Chapter 2 the adult's main concern at this time is to create the setting, and to 'accompany' the children in their learning journey assisting this in as personal a way as possible.

Examples of sample activity sessions

From sessions to lessons, from noticing to observing, from helping to challenging are important differential perspectives which face educators of young children. What follows now are two movement activity sessions related to two of the four categories of movement set out in Chapter 1.

The first *relates* to *a stable environment* and describes a situation which might arise spontaneously with, or be specifically planned for, children up to four years of age. Several individuals and groups of people will be involved in, and take responsibility for, movement activity sessions of the kind suggested here. They will all have some direct or indirect teaching component in what they do but the definition and extent of this will vary greatly according to the particular group of children and the context in which the activity occurs. This could be in the home, or in a variety of group settings, ranging from family units and early childhood settings through to infant and junior schools.

The second activity relates to children of about six and seven years, and is based on children's interest in *handling objects and making them move*. In each of the examples the teaching and learning situation is identified in the following terms:

- type of situation
- resources
- approximate age of children
- duration of activity
- learning phases
- challenges
- adult roles.

The most important resource of all, the adult who takes responsibility for the learning process, is involved in a variety of teaching strategies. These range widely from individually oriented involvement in the early activities of the youngest children right through to the class teacher or the movement specialist in the junior school. The strategies include:

- the making of suggestions and adult and child challenges
- observations and recording of general and specific kinds
- looking and talking with the children
- implementation of learning phases.

Session 1: movement activity related to a stable environment

Resource	Climbing frame with poles, ladders, planks, slides.
Age	Around four years.
Time	Fifteen minutes or as long as interest lasts.
Learning phase	Free exploration.
Challenge	Children encouraged to use the apparatus as they like.
Role of adult	To observe and comment generally and with individual children about what they are doing.
	To draw attention to parts of the body and actions being used as they move.
	To select two activities to be shown.
	For example, looking with the children at the following:
	• one child travelling along the plank on the 'tummy' pulling along with hands

	• another child climbing the frame using hands and feet.
Looking and talking	Children, are asked to identify, name and talk about:
	• parts of the body being used
	• different ways these are used, e.g. to pull along or climb.
Challenge	Children asked to go back to where they were working, to move again in their 'special' way.
	To make it clear what parts of themselves they are using and what sorts of actions they are doing. They may like to name the body parts and actions to themselves as they go along.
Learning phase	Consolidation.
Role of adult	To observe and talk with the children about what they are doing.
	To select two further examples and ask children to comment emphasising body parts and actions.

Session 1 reviewed

Underlying a decision to work with young children in this way is the assumption that, at certain periods during the day, it is important for young children to have the opportunity to spend some time on agility-type apparatus whether at home, at the play group, with the childminder or at nursery school. It is a case of seizing the opportunity, of finding an appropriate period of time to become actively involved in the children's learning. The appropriateness relates both to the children and to the adult who has to fit this in amongst the many other calls upon time, energy and attention.

We have seen from the activity chart above that the first task is to observe what the children are doing and how the information, gleaned from these observations, can best be used. This involves the teacher making a mental assessment as the child travels around. Having decided on the movement ideas most in evidence, two examples can then be selected. Children of this age are not always able to reproduce on request what is wanted, and it is a good idea to ask them to try to remember what they are doing because it may be shown to the other children later on. In this case, the two examples – and they are only examples – of travelling along the plank on the tummy and climbing the frame using hands and feet, were chosen.

The body with all its various connotations is an early and recurring frame of reference for young children. In looking at the two activities the children

are asked to name and talk about body parts involved and the actions performed. This gives them two things to keep in mind, which, because they are
closely related, is just about right for children of this age. It is not chance that
the two activities selected to be shown were very different from each other
both in terms of the parts of the body involved and in the ways of moving.
This allows ideas about 'different from' to be used to help the children
describe the activities they were watching or doing.

In the second, consolidation, phase, the activity chart shows that the children are given a chance to concentrate once more on 'me and my movement'. This time they will be able to do this with greater understanding and
clarity because of the shared looking, naming and describing activity which
has just taken place. The ability of the adult to move around the group consolidating what has been, and is being, learned is an important part of the
session. The time allocation of 'as long as interest is maintained' reflects the
fact that with these young children much of what goes on is an individual
affair which may be longer and more concentrated for some individuals than
for others.

*Session 2: handling objects and making them move: versatility and skill in
games*

Resource	Balls, bats, sticks, hoops, ropes, bean bags, rings, cones, etc.
Age	Six to seven years.
Time	Thirty minutes.
Challenge	Children asked to collect the apparatus they were using at the end of the previous lesson and practise the activity they had made up.
Learning phase	Consolidation (apparatus being used and activity established).
Role of adult	To travel round class and comment to individuals and to make general comments to class.
	To look at two or three activities and discuss with children in terms of what are the difficult parts, what individual children are doing well and what might help to make it even better.
Challenge	Children to return to their activities remembering the inherent 'help-hints' they had talked about.
Learning phase	Consolidation.

Challenge	Children asked to choose different apparatus this time and to find 'unusual' ways to make it move.
Learning phase	Guided exploration.
Role of adult	To observe and encourage individuals to experiment with 'out of the ordinary' parts of their bodies to make the apparatus move. To anticipate the selection of two children. For example:
	• one child moving on front of body using his head to make the ball travel
	• a second child jumping with bean bag between his feet.
Looking and talking	Discussing the skills involved in the two activities:
	• amount of control in keeping ball close to head
	• giving the body two jobs – to grip the bean bag between the feet and to jump well.
Challenge	All children encouraged to make their activities more skilled and be prepared to explain in words and movement how they are doing this.
Learning phase	Consolidation.
Challenge	Children to go back to the apparatus they were using at the start of the lesson and this time make up an activity where the apparatus goes either upwards or forwards.
Learning phase	Guided exploration (incorporating consolidation).
Role of adult	Selecting two contrasting examples.
	• one child with rope skipping forwards
	• another child throwing and catching a rubber ring upwards.
Looking and talking	Talking with the children about:
	• the difference in direction
	• the same body parts being used
	• different actions.

Session 2 reviewed

This session is directly structured and likely to exist as one of a series of lessons planned over a given length of time, perhaps four or five weeks. It takes into consideration the assumption that six- and seven-year-olds will be able to remember what they were doing in the previous lesson, although in some cases they may need some help. Secure in this knowledge the teacher can start with a phase of consolidation – in this case to ask the children to collect the apparatus they used the time before. In this reiterative process the role of the teacher is to enhance the learning of an already established activity. A second period of consolidation follows the observation and discussion of selected activities. This is more concentrated in nature and also presupposes that the children can transfer some of the 'help-hints' to their own activities.

The second challenge is carried out within the learning phase of guided exploration where the teacher encourages exploratory activity through the suggestion to choose different apparatus and to find unusual ways to make it move. Two things for the children to remember here: different apparatus and unusual ways of using it. Again two crucial strategies are used: the selection by the teacher of relevant activities and the use made of these by looking and talking together about them. As in the previous lesson the teacher has picked out two very different activities to show the class and to form the basis of discussion. On this occasion it would have been just as valuable to have selected two activities which had components in common, thus extending thought in a classificatory rather than a discriminatory context.

Following a further phase of consolidation the children are prepared for one last task which is to return to the apparatus they were using at the start of the lesson but this time to make their apparatus go up or forwards thus introducing a spatial, trajectory element to their game. It is vital that sufficient time is allowed for the children's responses to this challenge. In the time allotted to looking and talking together the children are asked to analyse two games, one going forward while skipping and another showing the upward throwing and catching of a rubber ring. These two distinctly different games activities are quite complex. In addition to highlighting the directional differences the teacher takes the opportunity to identify the skill factors needed in each. The lesson ends with the children reworking their games in the light of comments made.

Starting, supporting, checking and recording

Concentration on ways in which children's movement education can be supported, extended and enriched culminates here with a list of suggestions which may be given to children from three to eight years; to individuals, small groups or classes in either formal or informal situations.

The list is a 'sample' collection of suggestions from one area of movement only, namely agility. It is suggested for 'short-term loan' only for the advantage of the movement classification is that, once thoroughly digested, many, many more such lists may be collated for any type of movement activity. This particular collection starts with just one, and then two, movement ideas which develop in complexity in what is being asked of the children.

In the first instance, the object is to provide some suggestions from which parents and early childhood educators can select what they think is most relevant. However, the list has other uses. It makes it possible to check for areas of movement not given recent attention perhaps levels, or symmetry, or patterns. To check when these suspected omissions were last considered should simply be a task of looking back through the records. Records might show that certain areas have been overused and that well-established and repeated patterns of movement need enlarging and developing along with the implementation of new ones. Importantly the suggested movement content could reinforce and 'flesh out' the dominant schemas being used elsewhere in the home, the play group, the nursery or the school. A child who seems completely absorbed in 'over and under' behaviour may benefit from an immersion in movement situations which provide opportunities of a similar nature which will 'aid and abet' this particular aspect of learning (Athey 1990).

The listed challenges do not have to be used as they appear here, as predetermined ones, and they can be even more open-ended. Alternatively, they can provide a basis from which to assess what is happening in young children's movement; instead of suggesting that children try out certain tasks, the content of those tasks could be a focus of observation. Which children are finding lots of places to jump? Are there examples of children travelling backwards? Who, for days now, has been showing delight in going up and down everything in sight? Adults have a lot to offer in following up these observations by means of supporting and extending them as well as 'spotting' activities which are just emerging or are beginning to be shared.

Children enjoy responding to movement challenges wherever they happen to be. Sometimes they challenge themselves, sometimes they appreciate adults setting challenges and they frequently enjoy setting challenges for each other. The following activities may be those we can see happening freely all around us, or they can form the basis of adult-led experiences.

ACTIVITY	MOVEMENT FOCUS	LEARNING IMPLICATIONS
Jumping being practised in one place	**Body**: action	Need to do activity over and over again – carrying out jumping schema
Stretching the body fully while moving forwards	**Body**: action and shape **Space**: direction	Two things to be held in mind
Moving on the apparatus using only **hands and feet**	**Body**: parts emphasised and parts restricted	Encourages invention
Travelling round the room with **one part** of the body **leading the way**	**Body**: part leading	As one body part leads the rest of the body needs to 'line up'
Movement where **both sides of the body** are doing **the same thing**	**Body**: design	Sense of symmetry and balance
Balancing on **different parts** of the body	**Body**: action and parts taking weight	Alignment of rest of the body according to points of balance
Climbing in lots of **different places**	**Body**: action	Finding different situations where climbing schema can be used
Moving on floor/apparatus on **hands** and **feet** travelling in one direction	**Body**: part highlighted **Space**: direction	Keeping two things in mind: (a) the body and (b) the space
Going **under** and **over** the apparatus with some things happening **slowly**, others **quickly**	**Space**: zone **Dynamics**: time	Concentration on the 'how' and 'where' of movement
Lots of activities on the floor **without putting weight on feet**	**Body**: restriction of parts	Emphasising invention in terms of bodily agility
Finding ways of **passing each other**	**Relationship**: with partner	Having to adapt to partner, to negotiate, to share a common goal
Playing **follow my leader**	**Relationship**: duo – leading and following	Adapting to leader's actions, pathway and timing

Figure 21   A sample list of agility challenges

Summary

Children learn in situations which are neither undemanding nor overwhelming. We can use what we know about the process of learning to help children to build on what they already know, giving them opportunities to struggle, practise and play.   (Roberts 2002: 82)

6

A matter of expression

Your body is your language. Cultivate your language. Be able to say what you want.
(Holm 1980: 81)

One of the major aims of adults working with young children is effective and sensitive interaction. This arises spontaneously to match particular occasions and also takes place over longer periods of time. However good and extensive provision for learning may be, however effectively each day is organised, however informed the 'curriculum', interpersonal relations are of prime importance. Being in tune with children's thoughts and feelings is essential for maximum development in all areas of learning and at all developmental sequences.

Establishing the boundaries

As we turn now to look at the way in which children's movement is linked with emotional and expressive behaviour it is important to stress that this chapter does not address personality theories. Neither is it concerned with body language theories, many of which are well-researched collections of signs and signals carrying prescribed meanings. Instead, we are concerned with the stream of movement occurrences as we look at the part movement plays in the expression of personality or, put another way, at how expressive behaviour can be assessed in movement terms. North (1972: 12) writes:

> *If we accept that the way people sit, walk and make gestures has any relevance to how they are thinking and feeling, then it is only a short step towards the idea that a more subtle and deep analysis of the composition of the movement can lead towards a greater understanding of the personality.*

It is also important to stress that this book does not intend to look at the complexity of the observation and interpretation of movement phrases and clusters or of the in-depth study of human movement itself. Those wishing to learn more should refer to the works of Laban and Lawrence (1947), Lamb

(1965), North (1972), Sherborne (1990) and the many educationalists, therapists and movement specialists who have contributed to this immense field of study. Too numerous to mention here, their publications feature throughout the text and are included in the Bibliography.

North (1972: 12) suggests: 'It is common knowledge that we are all observers of movement, and that we all draw conclusions from our observations of other people.' She indicates that there is much that can be done by the non-specialist in this field. Writing in the field of movement expression Lawrence (1947: xv), an industrialist who worked with Laban, agrees with North and suggests:

> To be a good observer of other persons' effort-expressions, one need not oneself have great bodily expressiveness. Good movers may be poor observers.

Those concerned with the care and education of young children are already tried and tested in the art not only of looking but also of seeing. As Lally (1991: 87) (Edgington) points out, 'teachers and nursery nurses are trained both to observe and to learn from observation' and are constantly intent on improving their practice.

All movement is expressive

All movement, however small, is a means of expressing and communicating. The expressive nature of movement applies to both descriptive gestures and utilitarian tasks and is an important component of the learning process. Through a repertoire of personalised movement patterns, children, their parents and teachers show themselves as unique individuals. Although young children employ highly differentiated combinations of movement ingredients, there are some elements that are fairly common to specific situations. Children adopt similar patterns of waving; they nod and shake their head using common directions; they embrace and kiss in roughly the same way. But even within those common patterns there are clearly observable cultural and social norms, as well as individual differences, all of which play their part in shaping what takes place.

Moods and movement

Movement does not, by any means, tell everything we may wish to know about the things children are attempting to express or communicate.

However, as one type of indicator, it is an invaluable contributor. An important point made by Whitehead (2002: 5) is that movement acts as a support system of nonverbal communicative signals which can be added to our use of linguistic and prelinguistic indicators. As well as individual shapes and shadings which contribute to the uniqueness of each individual, there is a range of dynamic forms and patterns common to most children in the expression of moods such as anger, excitement, anxiety and distress and it may be helpful to look at these first. On occasions early childhood practitioners will have seen children engage in moments of an expressive nature along the following lines:

- jumping for joy
- shaking with excitement
- inching forward cautiously
- holding back with reticence
- hitting out in anger
- slumping in dejection
- bursting with pride
- rising to the occasion
- digging in their heels
- throwing themselves wholeheartedly – or whole-bodily – into the game.

By looking at these examples we can see that through actions (jumping and shaking) and body parts (heels and toes) the **Body** clearly remains a central feature of expressive activity. In terms of **Space**, directions such as *forward, backward, upward and downward* are there along with their spatial counterparts of *rising and sinking, advancing and retreating*. However, **Dynamics**, the qualitative element indicating *how* the activities are dynamically charged, is more implicitly conveyed. Reticence and caution imply restraint through the presence of bound flow. Hitting out suggests strength as does the digging in of heels. The excitement of jumping for joy could be said to be tinged with a sense of lightness, even light-heartedness. **Relationships**, in these examples, are also a matter of implication. There could be someone at the receiving end of hitting out while the reticent withholding may be in relation to a stranger who had just appeared on the scene.

   There is no doubt that in Photograph 52, Jade, aged four, seen on the far left, is expressing pride at her accomplishment in the informal race which had just taken place. It would be easy to assume that she was the winner. In fact she came second! In this case the pride and expression of self-esteem is simply associated with having taken part.

Photograph 52   Jade the proud participator

Making a note of it

There are more descriptions in everyday use which carry movement connotations than we perhaps first imagine. Newspapers, journals, reviews, and character portraits in literature, are full of such examples. Parents and professionals alike use movement endowed phrases to describe the children in their care. In the context of early childhood education, such descriptions which include comments on movement expression give insight and under-standing. Making notes of consistent as well as irregular and unusual move-ment-stressed occurrences is an important way of recording expressive movement behaviour and, over a longer period of time, its development. In the first instance this can be done by recording very simple and uncompli-cated expressions of mood and feeling states such as resentment, tenderness or excitement. Information about the number and nature of significant expressive situations in respect of individual children can be swiftly assembled. Gathering of data of this kind will eventually result in building an informative picture of individual children and the interpretative outcomes can be used as part of a holistic profile. As Hodgson (2001: 173) notes:

> *Learning to see and notice movement from broad impression down to the finest detail is the important beginning to any greater understanding. Making mental and written notes will help the process and start the awareness of its fundamental nature.*

Personal style

Parents and early childhood educators will recognise that moods and feelings shown by one child will not necessarily be the same as those shown by their peers or siblings although there may be common components. It is not the case that anger always produces tightening of the muscles and hard-hitting action while happiness is expressed by large, exuberant and expansive movement. Among any set of children may be those whose expression of happiness is quiet and still and those whose anger may be cool and contained or wild and loose-limbed. To suggest that specific movement equals feeling would be a mistake. It would dismiss the whole idea of personal style and its relationship to social and cultural norms. North (1972: 35) summarises in this way:

> *It is impossible to say either that a particular movement equals a special quality or that a special quality equals one movement pattern ...*

Different contexts also bring out different movement expression although over lengthy periods of observation these are usually seen to arise from and be part of the general movement repertoire of a particular child. The following observations show two different ways in which Jason expressed himself in movement terms. Importantly, reasons for these particular modes of expression are also suggested.

Diary notes

Date
Mood/expressive activity
Excitement – high level of agitation – seen on and off throughout the day. Rushing around boisterously. Changing from one action to another; running, jumping, spinning, jigging up and down. Laughing loudly.

Comments
It is his fourth birthday and he is having a party when he gets home.

Date
Mood/expressive activity
Temper tantrum – on arrival. Tight body, clenched fists, stamping feet. Clung hard to mother and dragged right back from her as she brought him through the door. He didn't communicate with anyone at first but the tension temporarily eased building again towards the end of the day.

Comments
Most unusual behaviour – difficult to know why this happened. He did have one set back yesterday when he couldn't use the slide when he wanted. When he collected Jason, his father explained that Jason wanted to accompany his parents who were going to visit his grandparents for the day. Jason often stayed overnight when he went to visit and he was probably worried in case his mother and father didn't get back in time to collect him.

Perry and Jake: movement expression in context

In the momentary absence of swans and geese on the river, two-and-a-half-year-old Perry spent a busy time feeding the pigeons which gathered regularly on the bridge. His movement was generally outgoing and free as he 'pursued' them with his bread. Then suddenly he saw a swan and for one moment sheer excitement made him stop absolutely still in his tracks. His body narrowed and all parts came immediately to his centre. His hands covered his mouth, his eyes almost closed, and even his toes appeared to turn up as, seeming to hug the excitement to himself, he looked at the swan – the pigeons for the moment forgotten. His special moment of excitement and delight shared by his family, and seen in Photograph 53, were soon replaced by his previous boisterous, action-packed behaviour as he returned again to his friendly pursuit of the pigeons. Although Perry's expression is clear and meaningful, in a different context it could have signified something different.

Photograph 53   Excitement shown by Perry, aged two

In the case of Jake, aged five, excitement is expressed in a quite different way as he achieves the moment of greatest height on the see-saw. His total body attitude is one of expansion, his legs are wide astride, his chest is wide open – and his mouth too! The mood is one of large, freely flowing joy. The only sign of restraint and binding of flow is an appropriate one as Jake controls his position on the see-saw with his hands.

Photograph 54   Excitement shown by Jake, aged five

Examining the link between movement and feeling Borton (1963) writes, in poetic vein, about the variety of expression which can be associated with moving backward:

> *Backward-going movement can shrink in fear,*
> *recoil in disgust, or spring back in surprise.*
> *It can be as stingy as a miser's closing fist*
> *or as cold and unsociable as an oyster*
> *drawing into its shell. When I move backwards,*
> *I am a cat cringing in terror ...*
> *or a flower closing its petals against the frosty night air.*

And moving forwards:

> *Forward-going movement can be open*
> *and giving ... but it can push and take*
> *too, like a child grabbing toys from*
> *his playmate. It can be sassy as*
> *a stuck-out tongue, or as impulsive*
> *as a leap in the dark. It can be as*
> *bold as a punch in the nose, or*
> *as menacing as a tidal wave.*

Most, but not all, children express themselves freely and fully. They leave little doubt about how they feel in the minds of those 'in charge' or those who just happen to pass through their sphere of expressive activity. At certain times, and with some children, the movement expression is less obvious and it is necessary to look more closely in order to decipher the messages being unconsciously, or intentionally, conveyed. But, whether full blown or understated, the movement phrases of young children, and the colourful analytical phrases with which they are described, are clearly articulated.

The classification of movement re-visited

In order to delve a little deeper into the significance of the relationship between children's movement and their emotional and expressive development we need to have the four categories of movement in the forefront of our minds. It would be helpful, therefore, to look back and refresh memories of the original classification in Chapter 1 which gives detailed information about:

- *what* moves – the body
- *how* it moves – the expressive quality involved
- *where* it moves – within and outside its own special space
- *with whom or with what* it relates – the people and objects which fill the day.

How children move: making an 'effort'

Of special importance is the second section of the classification which refers to *how* children move. Hodgson (2001: 183) points out that one of the most important aspects of Laban's awareness of movement is his recognition that movement has a quality which according to Preston-Dunlop (1998: 277) is:

> *created by preferences in how that person responds to the world: that is how he or she behaves. Such patterns are unique to each individual, and seen in the differences of timing, of weight use, of spatial patterning, and flow that a person exhibits.*

Attention was drawn in Chapter 1 and subsequent chapters to the ways in which movement is dynamically charged and structured and suggestions made as to how movement needs to be appropriately coloured in order to be both effective and expressive. However, because this part of the classification is especially relevant to the expressive and emotional make-up of young children it is given additional consideration within this chapter. At this point another look at the four motion factors of weight, space, time and flow, introduced in Chapter 1, may prove helpful.

Weight

The weight factor of movement gives rise to a fine, sensitive manner of moving at one end of the continuum through to one of strength and firmness at the other.

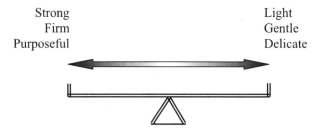

Strong   Light
Firm   Gentle
Purposeful   Delicate

Figure 22 The weight factor continuum

Because the weight factor is associated with actual tension in the muscles, it is sometimes called the physical component. It is associated with *intention*. In general terms one person can be heard to say of another 'she takes a firm stand' or 'he only touched lightly on that subject'. Each of these comments says something about people acting in certain situations just as the following observation says something about three-year-old Alison when she was called in from the garden where she was playing. She folded her arms, plonked her feet apart and said '*No*' firmly and loudly, indicating that she had every *intention* of staying just where she was.

Qualitative space

The space factor of movement gives rise to elements of flexibility through to directness. This motion factor is linked with *attention*. One end of the continuum is associated with the capacity to home in or to pinpoint while at the other end there is a flexible all-roundness in the expression indicating consideration of all sides of a situation. Sophie, aged two, illustrates this well for us. When she is painting, a special interest of hers, she is quite unaware of all the other things going on around her. She gives her painting her undivided *attention* until she wants to do something else. This narrow focusing was seen earlier in Photograph 6 (Chapter 1) which shows Mark totally engrossed in his model-making.

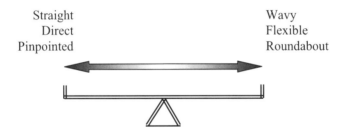

Straight   Wavy
Direct   Flexible
Pinpointed   Roundabout

Figure 23 The qualitative space factor continuum

Time

Time, the third motion factor, is associated with *decisiveness* and the range of expressive activity travels between degrees of suddenness and sustainment.

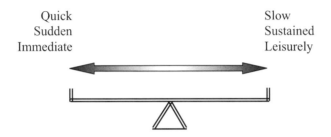

Quick   Slow
Sudden   Sustained
Immediate   Leisurely

Figure 24 The time factor continuum

Sudden, abrupt, quick movement is typical of those people who act and react with immediacy, while leisure and unhurried pace are characteristic of those who take a long time to come to a decision or judgement of any kind. Tariq, aged five, and at infant school, displays a strong sense of suddenness. When his teacher asks a question Tariq is always ready to leap in with the answer. He does not pause to think before deciding to respond and he sometimes forgets what he wants to say – that is, if he always has something ready to say in the first place!

Flow

Flow, the last of the four motion factors, is the most complex one. This is because it has a dual role. It is linked on the one hand with *precision* of action and, on the other, with *communication*.

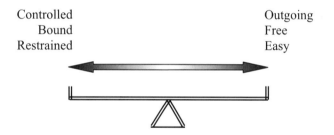

Controlled	Outgoing
Bound	Free
Restrained	Easy

Figure 25 The flow factor continuum

Flow is concerned with the care and control used in carrying out everyday acts. It is also about the making, breaking and withholding of relationships. Free flow is characterised by the outgoing nature of movement, with ease and lack of restriction, and bound flow by a certain stickiness and caution. There is no sign of stickiness or caution in Gavin's behaviour. He is a good communicator. He loves being with people and people enjoy being with him. Whenever anyone new comes into the nursery he is among the first to get acquainted.

At this point it is worth reiterating the value-free nature of movement elements in their own right. Only if they are used inappropriately, or in an exaggerated manner, can they be said to be negative. All children have natural preferences and it is these sets of preferences which give them their individuality.

Assessing expressive behaviour

Central to the concept of motion factors is that movement takes place on a continuum rather than being seen as two polarities such as 'sudden' and 'sustained'. The sense of being moderately sustained, extremely sudden or hardly registering a time sense at all – that is, operating in a somewhat neutral area – are all possibilities of differentiation. Important, too, is the implication that movement can range between and within personal limits.

Trained movement observers would be able to establish fine degrees of differentiation as to where on each of the 'continuums' individuals are functioning. Most importantly, they would then relate these to the other three factors, namely, the body, the space and relationships. Such detailed observations, along with their interpretations, would be of particular significance to educational psychologists and therapists working with clients needing specialist help. However, there are relevant and relatively simple means of assessing the expressive status quo of young children in terms of movement which can be used effectively by all early childhood educators and which will support the general compilation of records.

The following movement profiles of Shobana, aged three, and Timothy, aged five, use observations related specifically and exclusively to the four motion factors of weight, time, qualitative space and flow. The four 'markers' used in making the placements are:

↔   the range of movement expression

▨   the extent to which a quality is experienced

○   the extent to which the complementary quality is experienced

Δ   the fulcrum signifying a somewhat neutral area. The nearer
     movement is to the fulcrum the less pronounced it is.

Shobana's movement profile

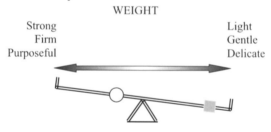

WEIGHT

Strong	Light
Firm	Gentle
Purposeful	Delicate

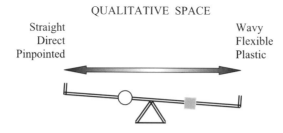

QUALITATIVE SPACE

Straight	Wavy
Direct	Flexible
Pinpointed	Plastic

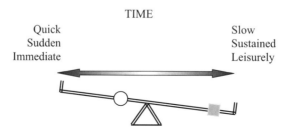

TIME

Quick	Slow
Sudden	Sustained
Immediate	Leisurely

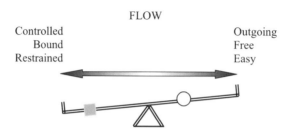

FLOW

Controlled	Outgoing
Bound	Free
Restrained	Easy

Figure 26   Shobana aged three years: a 'dynamic' movement profile

What do the observations in Figure 26 tell us about Shobana's movement?

(a) Shobana moves very gently. She is extremely delicate in what she does (near the end of the continuum). However, in contrast, she has very little at her disposal in terms of strong and forceful qualities. Note that her placement in terms of strength is only just the other side of the fulcrum.

(b) In terms of spatial quality, Shobana shows that she is able to perform with considerable degrees of flexibility, although there is still plenty of room for development. In comparison with her performance within the weight factor she has a slightly less extensive range. Her ability to carry out direct and straight movements is fairly limited (near the fulcrum).

(c) Shobana's attitude to the time factor almost exactly resembles her weight factor. She is predominantly a slow, sustained mover with little evidence at this stage of being able to produce much in the way of quick, abrupt movement.

(d) In terms of flow the emphasis of Shobana's movement is restrained and tightly controlled. Her ability to be free and more abandoned, as shown by her nearness to the fulcrum, is minimal.

Having made a current record of Shobana's qualitative movement range, we can now check to see if these observations relate to the recording of other activities in which she participates. The following movement observations were made of Shobana in her participation in domestic play and outside activities. This is what was found.

Shobana: domestic play

Shobana spent some time looking round trying to choose what to do. She eventually decided to wash and dress her family of dolls. She handled each one of them with care, not being rough when she washed them and combing their hair carefully and gently. The movement clues to take account of in this description are:

Weight: The *intention* stress was in the gentle, sensitive handling of the dolls with no sign of roughness.

Qualitative space: A flexible *attention* was seen in her looking around while considering what to do. Then she directed *attention* to the task in hand and kept her concentration fixed.

Time: A leisurely *decision* – she took her time.

Flow: Care and precision characterised the *control* which was exercised in combing the doll's hair.

Shobana: outside activity

Shobana expressed a wish to skip and was guided to where the ropes were kept. After a few minutes trying to make the rope go over her head she gave up – she 'did not really want to do it' she said. After wandering around the play area she eventually decided to use the slide. Ian, impatient with her slow ascent up the ladder, tried to push in front. Shobana just allowed herself to be pushed aside and, as was often the case with Shobana at this stage, there was no attempt to stand up for herself. She seemed quite upset and it was some time before she cautiously approached a group of children who were gardening. Although there was no apparent problem, she did not really communicate with them and played on the outskirts of the group. In terms of Shobana's outdoor activity we can see the following evidence of movement expression:

Weight: There were two instances where she lacked a sufficiently strong intention. The first was in really getting to grips with her skipping. She made only a light-hearted attempt. The second was in not taking a strong stand when Ian pushed in front of her.

Qualitative space: Again Shobana looked at what she would do next before she gave the slide – and later the children – her attention.

Time: There was nothing quick about her *decision* to use the climbing frame and although she did not stay around neither did she rush away from the scene of confrontation. She was slow to recover from Ian's intervention and took her time before going to join the children gardening.

Flow: Shobana did not *communicate* freely with the children she joined, preferring to 'keep herself to herself'.

Timothy's movement profile

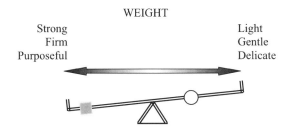

WEIGHT

Strong   Light
Firm   Gentle
Purposeful   Delicate

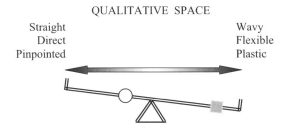

QUALITATIVE SPACE

Straight   Wavy
Direct   Flexible
Pinpointed   Plastic

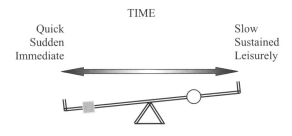

TIME

Quick   Slow
Sudden   Sustained
Immediate   Leisurely

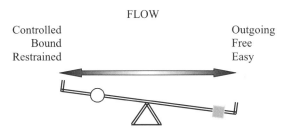

FLOW

Controlled   Outgoing
Bound   Free
Restrained   Easy

Figure 27   Timothy aged five years: a 'dynamic' movement profile

What do these observations in Figure 27 tell us about Timothy's movement?

(a) Timothy's movement patterns show strength – he moves with purpose. Although slightly less developed than his firmness, he shows a good degree of more delicate, sensitive movement. In fact within the weight factor he shows a good range.

(b) Spatially Timothy is more flexible than direct. The reasonably well-developed plasticity of movement is not complemented to the same degree by the linear, straight aspect.

(c) Timothy's time range is wide. Although he shows a slight preference for sudden, abrupt movement he is also able to move with a slow, more leisurely quality.

(d) In terms of flow, Timothy has a good capacity for freely flowing, un-restrained, outgoing movement. He can also produce a controlled and precise quality although this is a slightly less developed area of expression.

A search is now made for supporting or conflicting evidence in descriptive passages of Timothy in different situations – in a dance session and outside in the playground.

Timothy: the dance lesson

The teacher, who was working with the children on the idea of 'a dance of the autumn leaves', suggested that the children should show how leaves are blown along the ground and into the air. Timothy went immediately into action, hurling himself about the room with great abandon which bordered on a lack of control. However, he showed remarkably good judgement in avoiding collisions, weaving himself in and out of the other children with great skill. When asked to stop he was among the first to do so. When explor-ing being blown slowly and gently along the ground Timothy was able to manage this too. The movement correlations to take account of in this description are:

Weight: Implicit in the description of Timothy 'hurling' himself is the suggestion of strong *intention.* It almost gives the impression of being rough which can be a mis-use or exaggeration of strength. The description also tells us that Timothy is able to produce gentler movement.

Qualitative space:	The *attention* given to the flexibility of his body as he manoeuvred around the space and the other children reflected the thinking element connected with the space factor.
Time:	There is no doubt about Timothy's *decision* to move. It was abrupt and immediate. His response to the challenge to stop showed an equally quick response to the time factor. His ability to produce a slow, more leisurely quality shows that his range within the time factor is also quite well developed.
Flow:	The abandon with which Timothy set off signifies a personal delight in freely flowing, unrestrained movement where it could be said 'caution was thrown to the winds'. Like his strength, Timothy almost overdoes his free flow. One senses that with just a little more he would become 'out of control'. Yet we are assured that the *control* is there when necessary. The way in which he was able to 'put on the brakes' in order to avoid bumping into the other children showed that when he wanted he could employ considerable restraint.

Timothy: in the playground

Timothy seemed in constant demand on this occasion, with other children eager for him to play with them. He responded easily and quickly to them and, most of the time, seemed to join in sensitively with what they were doing. Occasionally he seemed to have to make his mark and was very tough with them. He got really angry. His interest did not last long and soon he was off somewhere else. The movement correlations to take account of here are:

Weight:	Leaving his mark indicates a certain power or strength in relating to the other children – his *intention* was to lead. There is a tendency here, shown also in the dance session, for his strength to be almost over the top. Such occasions seem to be sporadic, however, and he also shows sensitivity and gentleness.
Qualitative space:	This was not particularly emphasised in this situation.
Time:	Timothy's attitude to time was shown in swift and immediate action and reaction in *deciding* when to join and when to leave a group.
Flow:	His outgoing personality is a bonus in *communicating* with others. There is no feeling of holding back.

Linking records

Observations and records which concur with each other give additional sub-stance to the information base relating to individual children. Likewise, those which vary to any significant extent will provide scope for discussion, further investigation and consideration of short- and long-term plans for development. If movement observation and recording are new ventures for early childhood educators it may be worthwhile to start as a team. Observing a child's movement and discussing it is an excellent way of achieving a degree of objectivity and a sound way of establishing common principles. Drummond (1993: 150) gives a lead in this direction when she writes:

> *Trust and respect for each other's judgements will only develop when there are opportunities for open dialogue between teachers in different settings, opportunities for genuine debate and disagreement, as well as for agreement and accord. The dialogue will be concerned with the principles that underlie effective assessment as well as with the day to day practice.*

Movement observations of the kind used for Shobana and Timothy need to be made regularly but not too frequently – probably once or twice a month is about right. It is a good idea to have an observation sheet prepared, however, in case something remarkable occurs in between. Accounts from other areas of record-keeping will not always be so specifically 'movement conscious' as those for Shobana and Timothy. These were designed especially to show a maximum amount of possible connections to be made.

Movement implications within general record-keeping

Some 'non-movement specific' records will not suggest any explicit move-ment correlations at all. Others may pick out one very important, or perhaps recurring, characteristic such as this one taken from Bartholomew and Bruce (1993: 62):

> *Connor's lack of confidence makes him a bit tentative to approaching new activities – he needs adult encouragement to be drawn into different/novel situations – he loves things that are familiar e.g. he knows all about dinosaurs and feels very secure when holding forth about them. His approach to learning is a bit like his approach to strange food – he is highly suspicious and wary.*

In movement terms the whole of this most enlightening record draws atten-tion to Connor's bound flow. The operative words are *lack of confidence, ten-*

tative, suspicious and wary. However, free flow is obviously available to Connor, shown when dealing with familiar things. In this situation, as the record tells us, 'he is very secure'.

A similar record is provided by Edgington (Lally) (1998: 58) who writes of John, aged three years and ten months:

> *John was a gentle, articulate child. He was [also] very capable of attending to his own physical needs but he was less confident about using the nursery environment. He sometimes seemed nervous of some of the other children, particularly the more boisterous ones, and was unable to stand his ground if another child challenged him for a piece of equipment – in these situations he would let the other child have the toy and move quickly away from the area.*

As in Connor's case, this record tells of the presence of bound flow indicated in terms of him being 'less confident' and 'nervous'. There is no indication in this observation that free flow was one of his characteristics. But there are clues that, in terms of weight, he is considered to be a gentle boy (a positive statement) but that he was unable to take a 'firm stand' in the face of confrontation. His time sense is working well; he was quick to get away from the source of conflict!

The broader picture: a comprehensive movement profile

In this recent set of examples concentration has been on the dynamically emphasised category of movement, which plays a major role in expressive action. But, as confidence and skill in movement observation and recording grow, it is possible to look at small groups of clues, rather than single components. It is the relationship of all four motion factors – weight, space, time and flow – which gives the most comprehensive picture. Observations increase in meaning even more when the 'how' of movement is related to the other three categories of movement classification, namely, the body, the medium of space, and relationships.

The following movement profile of Peter, aged five, illustrates the way in which attention to all four categories of movement can be given. An analysis is provided in Figure 28 so that the movement implications can be easily recognised. Clearly, it is a fictional profile which has been constructed to include as many movement implications as possible. It does not refer to a particular individual and its place here is for illustrative purposes only.

DESCRIPTION		MOVEMENT IMPLICATIONS	
Stands on one leg with other foot turned in	→	BODY:	→ design – asymmetry
Lacks the drive	→	DYNAMIC:	→ weight – firm *intention* missing
Works slowly ...	→	DYNAMIC:	→ time – work pattern is slow and leisurely
And carefully	→	DYNAMIC:	→ flow – which is precise and controlled
A feeling of leisure	→	DYNAMIC:	→ time – a hint of being laid back
Examine the possibilities of various materials	→	DYNAMIC:	→ qualitative space – a flexible, wide-ranging *attention*
Focuses on the task in hand	→	DYNAMIC:	→ qualitative space – directs *attention* specifically to task
To work on the floor	→	SPACE:	→ level – low
Well away from any of the other children	→	SPACE:	→ keeps himself to himself
Rough and heavy-handed ... tightly	→	DYNAMIC:	→ weight – firm quality (mis-use)
Needs space to get over it	→	SPACE:	→ needs personal space, to be un-invaded
Usually sitting on the floor	→	SPACE:	→ level – low
Behind the door	→	SPACE:	zone – door in front of him, separating him from others or as protection
If anyone comes near him	→	SPACE:	→ personal space under threat
	→	RELATIONSHIP:	→ disallowed
Hits out at them	→	DYNAMIC:	→ weight – strong *intention*
	→	BODY:	→ action – hits
	→	RELATIONSHIP:	→ at other children
Curls up into a ball ...	→	BODY:	→ shape – all parts coming to the centre
Covering his face with his hands	→	BODY:	→ articulation – hands used to prevent contact
Holding his breath	→	DYNAMIC:	→ flow – bound (exaggerated use of restraint)
Gentler with animals	→	DYNAMIC:	→ weight – light and delicate handling
	→	RELATIONSHIP:	→ with animals
Stroking their fur	→	BODY:	→ action – stroking
	→	DYNAMIC:	→ weight – gentle (implied)
To relax him a little	→	DYNAMIC:	→ weight – release of strong tension
A similar gentleness	→	DYNAMIC:	→ weight – fine, light touch
Play tough roles ... clamping the cars	→	DYNAMIC:	→ weight – strong *intention*
Run and jump well	→	BODY:	→ action – run and jump
Control both the force ...	→	DYNAMIC:	→ weight – strong flow – bound/free precision
And direction of his kick	→	SPACE:	→ direction – to make it go where needed
Expert at dodging ... can twist and turn, while on the run changes direction easily	→	BODY:	→ action – can combine actions
	→	DYNAMIC:	→ qualitative space – channelled flow – fluent and free
Reticent and lacking in confidence ... not easy to talk to	→	DYNAMIC:	→ flow – bound, restrained, withdrawn
Few close friends ... keeps very much to himself	→	DYNAMIC:	→ flow – bound, cautious
	→	SPACE:	→ prefers personal space – not willing to let 'others in'
In one place in the room	→	SPACE:	→ prefers personal place
Signs of letting go ...	→	DYNAMIC:	→ flow – increase of free flow – out-going
Appears more expansive	→	BODY:	→ design – wider, more open

Figure 28   An analysis of the movement implications of Peter's profile

Peter's movement profile

Peter is fairly tall for his age, has a narrow chest, and frequently *stands on one leg with the other foot turned in*. He often *lacks the drive* to get the most out of a piece of work. He *works slowly and carefully* at his self-chosen activities, often with *a feeling of leisure*. In the use of scrap materials he has made several models and in each case he has been able to *examine the possibilities of the various materials* on hand in his attempts to make his models 'just right'. Having finally chosen what he needs he disregards the other things and *focuses on the task in hand*, preferring at this stage *to work on the floor* and *well away from any of the other children*. At the beginning of term, Peter was very interested in the hamster but was rather *rough and heavy-handed*, holding it *very tightly*. Sometimes Peter gets upset and after such occasions he needs *time* and *space* to get over this by himself, *usually sitting on the floor or behind the door. If anyone comes near him* at these times he *either hits out at them or curls up into a ball, covering his face with his hands and holding his breath*. Lately, he has been much *gentler with the animals* and spends a lot of time *stroking their fur*. This seems *to relax him a little*. He shows *a similar gentleness* when he takes on the role of father. It is interesting to note that he can also *play tough roles* as he does when he is the man *clamping the cars*. In his outdoor activities Peter excels. He can *run and jump well* for his age and is able to *control both the force and direction of his kick*. Above all, he is exceptionally *expert at dodging, he can twist and turn while on the run and changes direction easily*. Peter is making good progress but he still appears *reticent and lacking in confidence* at times. He is *not easy to talk to* and has *few close friends* although many of the children go out to him freely. He *keeps very much to himself* and prefers to work *in one place in the room*. However, through Peter's natural reserve, there are *signs of letting go* and he *appears more expansive* recently.

The purpose of detailed movement observation

Edgington (Lally) (1998: 126) maintains that effective observation of any kind relies on the teacher's ability to:

- observe each child as an individual and part of the group
- analyse and evaluate each observation
- identify the aspects of each observation which are significant in terms of the child's development
- use the information gained to inform her approach to each child.

Although the observation process itself is an interesting part of a teacher's role, it has no value unless it is put to use and fulfils its purpose as an educational tool. Nutbrown (1994: 149) agrees with Edgington about this and writes:

> *[Teachers] must create meaning from their observations and be prepared to use what they learn from these processes in their interactions with children.*

Purposeful observation specifically related to movement is not restricted to teachers. It helps all adults, in whatever capacity they function, to know the children better. It gives information about:

- children's personal movement style
- the range of dynamic expression
- preferred patterns of moving
- exaggerated areas of movement expression
- mis-used or inappropriate movement expression.

These are observation categories on which to build both short-term and long-term learning processes. Like all good learning, development starts from where the children are, using their arrival platforms for departures of all kinds. For the younger children, provision plays a large part. Timothy, who enjoyed the freely flowing, fast-moving 'autumn leaves' dance experience will learn to express different qualities and actions when moving with a balloon or to a piece of light, slow, lyrical music. Peter's tendency to 'hit out' may be used appropriately in a dance where the hands and feet first punch and disturb the air and are then used to smooth it down again. Much has been said already about suitable stimuli and appropriate provision and the theme will be taken up again in Chapter 7 which explores the notion of expression within the context of dance.

The 'movement repertoires' of parents, carers and teachers

Most occupations need a fairly extensive working movement vocabulary in order to carry out respective jobs with relevance and effectiveness. Teachers and carers need a wide span of movement expression. Coping with and responding to sometimes as many as twenty or thirty different 'personality styles' requires expertise. The adult may need to be sensitive to one child, take a firm stand with another, be aware of all the different things going on around while giving undivided attention to an individual, know when to hold back, give out, let things take their time or react immediately. The demands are many.

Other occupations also need a varied response. Take, for example, the 'lollipop' men and women who see a similar collection of children safely across the road. They, too, have to be appropriate in the ways in which they act and react. So what is the difference? Essentially it lies in the *context* which, for the road safety warden, is more limited in purpose and outcome and, therefore, more predictable. Different children have to be responded to, so too does the traffic flow and road conditions but the situation *is contained in space* (the crossing and immediate environment) and *limited in time* (arrivals and departures of the children). The teaching of older children, and of certain subject specialisms, similarly calls on less in terms of a wide range of movement expression. Certainly, the younger the children, and the freer the situation in which they function, the greater the variety of interaction between them and their carers and educators.

Bruce (2002: 4) reminds us that:

> *It has been well known for many years that new born babies are most attentive to human voices, faces and eyes. They will spend surprisingly lengthy periods of time just gazing into the eyes of their carers. Adults on the receiving end of this adoration invariably respond by gazing back, smiling, nodding and talking to the baby 'as if' they were conversing with an understanding partner. They frequently stroke the baby's face, chin and lips, perhaps to emphasise the physical sources of human speech.*

Children observe adults too

Young children are also experts at reading the non-verbal messages given out, sometimes voluntarily and sometimes involuntarily, by the adult and peer world by which they are surrounded.

Figure 29 is how David, aged four, describes his mother. He writes about actions and moods and conveys a convincing picture.

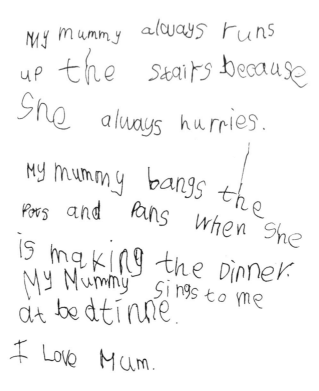

My mummy always runs
up the stairs because
she always hurries.

My mummy bangs the
pots and pans when she
is making the Dinner.
My Mummy sings to me
at bedtime.

I love Mum.

Figure 29   David describes his mother

Figure 30 shows what Amy, aged seven, has to say about her teacher. Notice the number of movement – and implied movement – references here and the way in which Amy contrasts moods.

Child-to-child interaction

Movement information can be used to advantage in supporting and enriching child-to-child interaction and communication. So often, it is the secure and confident children who are 'given' the new and diffident ones to look after and the quick reactors who are asked to help those who progress slowly. But when left to their own devices to whom do children most easily relate? Does movement profiling have a part to play here? Is there anything common to be found in terms of movement expression among those who habitually congregate together? Do children who are less often approached or included have anything in common? Certainly there is evidence to

My teacher is veay lively and is alway busy. She moves about like Roadrunner. she teaches us dance and every other class in the school. We have been doing Chinese movements and they are slow and calm. Our teacher cam move so slowly and softly. We all pretended to be gentle hovering birds. Mrs D also teaches us other subjects, maths, english, history, Science, art. We always do our beginnings of lessons sitting on the Carpet around her. She sits very still and talks to us calmly but if the topic is exciting She jumps about a lot again. Sometimes She is angry when people are naughty and She looks very cross. She bends her body over who she's really telling off but mostly she is happy. She smiles a lot and if something is funny She laughs.

Figure 30 Amy describes her teacher

suggest that children find companionship through the sharing of movement schemas. Nutbrown (1994: 17) enters into this debate suggesting that 'the question of whether schemas can influence children's choice of their partners in play is one needing further research'.

It may be a useful exercise to look occasionally at the movement characteristics shared, or not shared, in this way. This is not to encourage any sort of in-grouping or elitism, or to negate the fact that social development implies the ability to let go of self and relate to others. But, if the expressive qualities of the children are well known to the adults involved in caring and educating them, it should be possible to facilitate more appropriate 'sharing', 'looking after' and 'motivating' roles from time to time, as well as to encourage mixing and socialising in less familiar movement-shared relationships.

Summary

At the beginning of this chapter the point was made that movement does not tell us everything we need to know about each other. That remains true but there are times when movement can say more than words. On such occasions we should have the confidence to trust our feelings. In response to the movement cues which our children give us, a restraining hand, a fierce embrace, a hug, an encouraging nod, a shared smile may be all that is needed. If this is the case we should let it happen that way and then proceed from there.

7

Creating, performing and appreciating dance

Through dance the child can discover the body as an expressive instrument and develop the aesthetic and creative side of its nature.   (Hinkley 1980: 7)

Children as creators, performers and appreciators

Photograph 55   Dancing is a special sort of movement

Although there may be a few variations in the precise naming of the activities it is generally accepted that the triumvirate of *creating, performing and appreciating* dance as a conceptual basis underlies all phases of dance education. However, during the 1960s and 1970s the professional model, influenced by the world of professional dance, and the so-called child-centred framework, stemming from the ideas of Laban, existed as separate, and some-times opposing, approaches related to teaching dance in schools. The first of these featured significantly in secondary and tertiary education while the second retained a dominant position in the domain of primary education.

Nearly twenty years later and, as a result of much research in the field, Smith-Autard has presented a new theoretical model for the art of dance in education. Known as the Midway Model it focuses on:

> *dance in schools, colleges and universities which offer full-time education and form part of the national provision for compulsory education between the ages of five and sixteen ...*   (Smith-Autard 1994: vii)

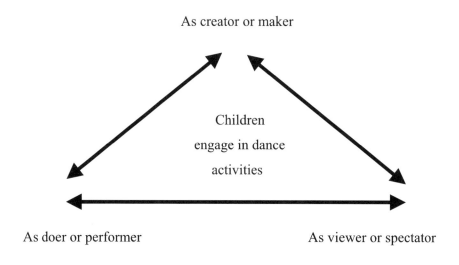

Figure 31   The dance roles in which children engage

The reorganisation and merging of the 'educational' and 'professional' models into the Midway Model has received much acclaim and is success-fully used in a wide range of educational settings. However, it could be argued that until recently, and with notable exceptions, the assimilation and practice of the model has been more effectively and extensively realised in secondary rather than primary, and especially early childhood, education. Therefore, although the model itself has become well established I strongly believe that:

the ways in which the notions and concepts within these areas can be applied to different cultures, styles and client groups are still relatively new. It is the relevant and appropriate application of the model which is the important issue now.   (Davies 1994: 73)

Identifying the nature of provision for the very young

In turning attention to the first phase of living and looking at what the three established 'roles' mean in the lives of young children, and of those who take responsibility for their learning, it is important to ensure that what takes place at secondary level is not simply watered down to cater for the younger children. It is also important to acknowledge that the understanding of child-centred education has undergone considerable change since the 1970s and increasingly encompasses developmental and subject-oriented under-pinning while maintaining the child at the hub of the equation.

The creative, performance and appreciation components now firmly in place in secondary education are also relevant for dance in the primary school. However, it is the ways they are perceived and operate that are different. In early childhood the three strands are especially flexible structures and carry several meanings related to young children's developmental sequencing. Performing can be taken to mean *'to do'*, *'to show'*, *'to dance'*, creating as *'making'*, *'trying out'* or *'composing'*, while appreciation is the outcome of *'watching'*, *'viewing'*, *'talking about'* and *'drawing about'* dance. It is also useful to remember that, in terms of aesthetic and creative education, dance has much to share with drama, music and the visual arts. There is a strong case to be made for dance in the home, early childhood settings or school to be catered for in a similar way to music and literature, for example, where the interdependent activities of making, doing, viewing and listening usually operate. In these subject-oriented areas it is important to note that children are not just restricted to creating their own sound compositions or making up their own stories. As well as being young *composers* or young *authors* they listen to music by a range of composers from different cultures and in different styles and on most days of the week hear a story read to them by their parents, carers, teachers or peers. In both these situations they become *appreciators*. When they tell or read their own stories or play their own sound compositions they become *performers*, with friends as a live audience always more than ready to offer advice and to become critic of the day.

Why then does making, doing and viewing happen less readily in dance than in music, painting, language or model-making? Why in so many statutory settings does it feature less prominently than the other arts? Does dance mean more in terms of organisation which perhaps acts as a deterrent? Clearing a space, gathering children together, making a journey to a special corner, room or hall and, in reception classes, helping them to get changed can seem like major events in an already full day. Some teachers may feel that their knowledge of the language of dance is inadequate or that help in introducing that language to young children is unavailable. With these probabilities in mind it may be helpful to look in some detail at how creating, performing and watching dance can occur with young children and function alongside the other artistic activities taking place.

The child as creator or dance-maker

Making and performing dance are often inextricably mixed. This is particularly so for young children whose dance is dancing and dancing is the dance. There is no magic formula which brings forth a dance-maker, or choreographer, at a particular age. There is no special moment when the mantle of choreographer is assumed. It is an activity which is built up gradually, and through a diversity of experiences, from an early age. As Hawkins (1964: 30) says, 'the creative aspect of dance should start early and be experienced continually'.

Helping children develop personal and interpersonal creativity in dance plays a central and pivotal role in early dance education. In essence it is concerned with appropriate structuring devices that can be used for developing dance creativity in young children and needs to take place within a broad framework which can be adapted as situations demand. There are important questions to be asked and answered here. What are these structuring devices? Do they facilitate or restrict? How should they be used? Should they be used at all with young children? Of course, we are not starting from scratch. There is plenty of written and photographic evidence to suggest that the creative process is in operation from a very early age. Sometimes it is the rhythm of what young children do which is all-important. Sometimes they find that the patterns they make are absorbing while at other times they are caught up in what their bodies can achieve or how it feels to be dancing with someone else. Young children's dancing is often full of contrast – at one time gentle and calm, at another fierce and stormy, for example, as it sweeps through the space, makes a bid for the sky and literally collides with the earth. It is a canvas of dance activity such as this that the children bring to their child-minders, their grandparents and to their nursery, infant and junior schools. It is a canvas which provides convincing evidence for the *raison d'être* of dance education. Harlow and Rolfe (1992: 16) write:

> It is the aim of dance education in the early years to foster and develop all these natural abilities by providing opportunities for pupils to create or compose simple dance sequences.

Helping the dance architecture take shape

In their dancing young children can often be seen going from one thing to another without making a conscious effort to build a repeatable dance. On such occasions they are not 'flitting' or lacking in concentration but rather allowing the different threads of their dancing to emerge and intertwine. This self-absorbing improvisation which is particularly characteristic of three- and four-year-olds will later play a part in more formal settings where exploratory dance-play comes into its own. When the time comes to help children with their dance-making there are several structuring devices which can be used effectively with young children. Two examples are given below and several more specific ways in which these may be used will be seen in the lessons associated with statutory education in Chapter 8.

Linking

One important choreographic device is the transition from one idea to another – the way in which movement ideas and activities are linked or juxtaposed. Perhaps the simplest illustration of this, and one which allows the maximum choice, deals with opposites, a notion that characterises the thinking of many young children. For example, making a *'quick and slow'* dance requires the children to make two appropriate passages of movement; one for the slow part, another for the quick part and designing a changeover between the two. Eventually, like a home-made song, the children can dance it again and again: it becomes their own composition. At the end of the day, it can be shown to family and friends in the same way as their paintings, stories and models. Unlike the paintings, stories and models, however, it is lost as soon as it ceases to be danced. The transitory nature of dance makes it difficult to keep ongoing records; unlike drawings and paintings they cannot be stored and reflected upon. However, this difficulty could be over-come to a certain extent if parents and early childhood practitioners kept photographic records or, better still, video scrapbooks, of the children's work.

A second, more complex, example of linking involves a tambour being played for the children in the following way:

- tapping the rim of the tambour with the end of the beater
- drawing the finger nails across the skin of the tambour.

The different sounds which emerge can first be explored separately as the children respond in their own ways to what they hear. The sound patterns can then be put into a sequence to help the children to create their '*tambour dances*'. As well as the structure being designed by the order in which the different sounds appear, the children are able to see the changes being made – which end of the beater is being used, or when the finger nails take over. Seeing, as well as hearing, is especially helpful for three- and four-year-olds in their initial attempts to structure experiences of this kind. Although the stimulus and the two-part structure are set, there can be as many outcomes as there are children in the group. It is an appropriate experience for children of different abilities and those with special needs, including wheelchair users. Linking continues as a transitional technique through all phases of dance education and can also be seen in a variety of video recordings of profes-sional choreography which teachers could show the children.

Association

Certain movement ideas frequently used by children in informal situations seem to belong together and can be utilised in dance. For example:

- running and leaping
- turning and twisting
- landing and rolling
- moving and stopping suddenly
- making straight and curved patterns
- reaching high and crouching low.

Exploration of phrases which have a natural kinship brings about a differen-tiation of rhythm in each case and an accompanying sense of mastery. Association can also come about through observation of a host of rhythmic and spatial structures in the environment with which young children identify and which are listed later on.

Dances cannot be made from nothing

Clearly, dance-making needs to have substance. It cannot exist in a void and it cannot exist without a language. Just as poetry needs words and sculpture requires substances like clay or wood, so dance composition needs movement. As children become more and more familiar with the language of dance – the material of movement – they slowly begin to differentiate between the process and the product. Unless they achieve familiarity with a wide range of movement expression, creativity cannot effectively take place. Instead, children will be seen to produce the same movements and movement patterns time and time again. Petricevic (1991: 253) puts it this way:

Children's imagination accepts no limits of expression but creativity is hindered by an inarticulate movement vocabulary.

An inarticulate movement vocabulary should not be confused with limited locomotion. It is possible to extend the movement vocabulary of all children whether paraplegic, using crutches or wheelchairs; for every child, however physically or cognitively challenged, to be involved in making dances.

Sources and resources

In addition to a rich and varied movement vocabulary, a range of sources and resources play an important part in the creative process. Ideas and stimuli can set off a whole spectrum of dance images which result in dance-play and dances. Apart from movement – the first and most readily available source of inspiration – there are many other sources which motivate children to dance and make dances. Within the confines of this chapter it is only possible to consider a few of these, and these only briefly.

The natural environment

This is rich in providing ideas for dance and giving it form. The actions and moods of the sea, the fish and plants which inhabit it, and the sand and rocks on which it breaks are full of dance images. Lots of action and qualities of movement stem from the observation of animals: cats that pounce, frogs and kangaroos that jump and snakes that slither and slide. More specifically, aspects of the weather can be used for structuring dance activity. For example, in different places at different times of the calendar year, winter conjures up many movement images: being blown by a strong, cold wind, skating on ice and alternately freezing and melting. Rain, a common feature of many countries, has a range of different qualities. It creates images of sprinkling, torrenting, relentlessness or sporadic appearance. *Storm* and *rainbow* dances involving small groups composing together can feature in the work of the seven- and eight-year-olds, while for the younger children individual *umbrella dances* and *jumping in and out of puddles dances* have their place.

Human-made structures

Whirligigs drying the clothes, mechanical toys, swings and roundabouts are all movement-invested happenings with which children, and adults, are familiar. Along with numerous other phenomena, they provide good starting points for dance. Fireworks are an admirable choice to help in dance structure. Throughout the southern and northern hemispheres there is a similarity in the movement and vocal expression of children who watch firework displays as there is in the shapes, patterns and sound effects of the fireworks themselves. The *firework dance*, considered at some length in Chapter 8, makes use of the three phases common to most fireworks – ignition, explosion and fade out – to provide both a stimulus and a structure for a dance arising from these visual and sound experiences. However, although a sequence of events may initially influence the structure of a dance such order does not necessarily have to be adhered to. Just as there is poetic licence there is also dance licence both in early childhood and at professional level where misalignment may be a deliberate choreographic strategy.

Sound

Self-expressed sound and movement make for interesting dance. Sound can encourage dance responses and can also accompany dance. The 'crackle' and 'pop' of the cornflakes, the 'revving up' of the engine and 'screeching' sound of brakes as the car rally is played out in the playground are part of the children's experience which can be used for dance. Photograph 56 captures a moment of a potential plane dance as it takes off, twists, turns and lands accompanied by a 'whoo' sound which elongates and shortens melodically and dynamically during the flight. This and similar activities reflect ways in which young children naturally accompany their movement with sound.

Photograph 56   The body tilts and the wings regulate as the plane turns

Action words

The human voice is an immediately available source used by adults to stimulate dance responses. Chapter 5 drew attention to the need for the teacher to match the quality of vocal sound to the content of the phrase. Action words and phrases can enhance or extend actions which children have in their repertoire but only if spoken with articulate relevance. Children love to make up their own action phrases ranging from the *'run and topple'* type of the three-year-olds to the more complex schema structures of the seven-year-olds in phrases such as *'cautiously creeping, silently stealing, bang, crash and far flung away'*.

A favourite activity of children aged about six, seven and eight is to accompany each other's dances with one child speaking the words while the other dances – a mixed-media duo. Even more interesting is to swap action phrases with each other. One child's action phrase of *'creep, crawl, pounce and catch'* contrasts quite distinctly with another's *'running, jumping and rolling along'*. The 'action swap shop' is a fun way for children to get on the inside of each other's dance and, in doing so, to extend their own dance vocabulary and sense of phrasing. This idea as a basis for a lesson can be seen in Chapter 8.

Poetry

Sometimes a poem is a good starting point. Two elements are important here. First, the poem should be short, possess a good helping of movement ideas and not be totally descriptive. Second, it must be well spoken or read. 'The Tide in the River' by Eleanor Farjeon is particularly suitable in length and content for younger children. There are not too many ideas on which to focus and the words suggest dynamic and spatial variety:

> *The tide in the river,*
> *The tide in the river,*
> *The tide in the river runs deep,*
> *I saw a shiver*
> *Pass over the river*
> *As the tide turns in its sleep.*

One of several ways to use this poem would be to take the three activities without the words and work with the children along the following lines:

- travelling smoothly and with change of level – going from high to low
- travelling smoothly, introducing a shiver which goes through the whole body
- making a big, slow, turning movement.

When the children have had time to make these activities their own, they may then be ready to perform them in accompaniment to the words. Using the poem in this way means that demands are not so exacting as to cause difficulties for the younger children and the framework provides a security which is not too rigorous.

Percussion

Percussion instruments relate well to dance. They can be used to stimulate, to accompany, or both. The range of sound which can be produced varies with the instrument. Different also are the responses to the sounds, as we saw in the tambour dances earlier. In playing the instrument themselves teachers can control the dynamics and shape of the phrase and have the freedom to modify it according to the responses from the children. When children handle percussion for their own dances they control their own phrasing although, because of the inherent challenges of managing to play and move at the same time, this is usually something which happens later usually at around seven or eight years. Too early an introduction for the children is likely to hamper both sound and dance expression.

Recorded music

Historically and artistically music is considered an established partner for dance and, perhaps, the most familiar one. It can provide rhythmic vitality, simple phrasing and lyrical or dramatic backcloths or atmospheres. However, with young children, there need to be some safeguards relating to its use for dance. With the youngest children aged between two and four years it is probably best to use it sparingly and in a highly selective way. Children in the early years are busy establishing their own rhythms and most find it difficult to conform to highly structured patterns not of their own making. It does not follow that music should never be used but that its selection should be carefully considered. There are three major ways which may be helpfully used in young children's dance:

- for improvisation and free response
- for the introduction and deepening of particular dance ideas
- for observation and follow up of children's spontaneous activities.

In the first of these a recording is played and the children respond without intervention of any kind, illustrating the learning phase of exploration discussed in Chapters 5 and 6. Such occasions give the children an opportunity to dance freely without restrictions, apart from the music, and even then they may at first continue dancing after it has finished! The second way concentrates on enriching and extending specific dance ideas which are currently being explored, for example, growing into a shape and shrinking back again or their articulated puppet dances. The third use of recorded music is to support the children's own dancing – to provide an appropriate backcloth against which their dancing can take place.

Touch

In their active exploration of the environment children are constantly touching and handling things. Touch often brings with it an almost instantaneous expressive quality of movement. Banging fists on the table, stroking the rabbit or the feel of dry sand running through fingers are just a few of the experiences involving touch which happen during the day. Many of these experiences can be given form and developed in the context of dance. One way of doing this is through linking the dance to the original action. The stroking action of the palms can be extended to involve the whole arm or two arms moving together. Stroking can be done with extreme gentleness and contrasted with a strong and energetic banging action, and strokes can be taken into different areas in space – in front, to the side and behind the body.

Clothes

It is well known that we are influenced by what we wear and that what we wear influences how we move. High heels and tight skirts bring about a different sort of self-presentation from jeans and a baggy sweater. The same applies to dance. The size, shape and weight of dressing-up materials all influence dance-making. They often set it off. Many a 'mysterious' dance has arisen from a long, black cloak, the same cloak which, on other occasions, has symbolised king-like qualities. Baggy trousers may suggest clowns or pirates, white scarves the clouds or snow. An extensive 'wardrobe' combined with appropriate dance themes allow gender issues to be opened up and for 'cross-dressing' to take its rightful place.

The child as performer

For the very young this may simply mean dancing. In this instance the term 'performance' gets its meaning from those who are watching rather than from performance aspirations on the part of the children dancing. For slightly older children it may signify dancing 'to' or 'for' another person, or a particular event. This entails the children 'showing' what they can do. Alternatively, showing may take place as part of sharing experiences. Showing is the non-verbal counterpart of telling. It should not be confused with 'showing off' with its attendant 'exhibiting' characteristics although a little of this may legitimately be present. For the two- and three-year-olds the performing role is often associated with dancing with those around them. 'Come and dance with me' is a frequently heard invitation. It is also one which can be given, in turn, by adults to individuals or groups of children. It can never start too young as shown in Photograph 57 where Zach, at twenty-seven weeks is dancing with Dad.

Photograph 57   Never too young to start: dancing with Dad on the deck

Young children carry their performance space around with them. It is thoroughly portable. It is the space where a dance is danced for the first time or where it is repeated. It can travel anywhere, the number of 'showings' depending on the depth and extent of interest on any given occasion. It may first be presented to the early childhood staff in the home corner, in the garden or kitchen to brothers and sisters on their arrival home from school and, later, to mother or father before bedtime.

A sense of venue

At an earlier age than might at first be imagined performance is seen as something more than dancing. The idea of performance usually incorporates a sense of venue. Almost every day, Kathryn, aged four, chose a tutu from the dressing-up clothes in the nursery, put on the cassette player and danced to the music. There was something over and above the personal love of dancing which was strongly present. This 'something' was an extra sense of performance seen in the way in which she prepared the dancing area for herself and responded to the children and nursery staff who sometimes stopped by to share the 'event'. Kathyrn attended ballet lessons twice a week and was already showing exceptional danceability. She was absorbed in her dancing and her dancing absorbed her. She danced for herself and any 'stop-by audience' was a by-product of her activity.

Tony, aged three, knew something about the components of performance but was not all together clear about the different roles involved. Although his family were present they did not feature prominently and his dance activity consisted of dancing around the room, clapping himself proudly and then drawing the curtains.

James, aged six, had a stronger concept of the performer–audience relationship involving several interrelated schemas. Taking some time in arranging the physical features of the venue he confidently set the scene. First, he drew the curtains across the windows in his bedroom and stayed still and quiet behind them while his family audience arrived and took their seats on the bed. His performance, which was a mixture of dance and drama, showed awareness of his audience and at the end of the show, after acknowledging the applause, he made his exit, drew the curtains behind him and waited for the audience to depart. Unlike Tony and Kathyrn, James's concept of a performance was pre-planned. He was able to predict, to hold several quite complex ideas in mind and carry out his plan of action.

Performance at school: the dance and skill dilemma

Once into the formalised setting of the infant school, children enter a situation where performing, alongside creating and viewing, becomes an important and well-articulated part of dance education. However, whenever the subject of performance in relation to young children is raised, so inevitably is the subject of skill. There are many and varied views on this issue. Williams draws our attention to children as performers being a dangerous aim of dance education unless it is fully understood. She warns that some teachers have preconceived models and 'instruct' the class in order for the children to achieve the necessary standards. She argues:

> *Dance is a performing art but it is erroneously considered that the degree of technical skill must be reasonably high before children can be engaged in the art form of the subject.*   (Williams 1988: 28)

This view appears, at first, to be countered by Harlow and Rolfe (1992: 15) who claim:

> *The mastery of basic skills is essential to enable them to move with ease and precision, allowing them to release their individuality in imaginative situations.*

However, the authors go on to suggest that mastery of basic skills refers here to an expanding dance vocabulary rather than just acquisition of particular bodily skills. Initially, they suggest, teaching should concentrate on bodily, dynamic and spatial aspects of movement. There is no doubt that the eloquence of performance reflects both the personal expressive characteristics of the children and the progressive development of these through an appropriate set of experiences.

Planned performance

Once children start statutory schooling the activity of sharing, which inevitably has something of a sense of performance about it, is different. Performance is now twofold and often intentionally incorporated into the teaching plan. First, it continues as a *participatory activity* where a group of children respond to suggestions, for example, to:

- move freely to the music
- creep, crawl, wriggle and flop.

In response to both challenges the children move individually and in concert with each other. In moving freely to the music a range of different instruments (*the children's bodies*) play different tunes (*their movement phrases*). In creeping, crawling, wriggling and flopping, different instruments (*the chil-*

dren's bodies) play the same tune (*the movement phrase*) but with individual, personal qualities.

Photograph 58 shows Richard, aged six, showing his creeping dance. We can see the cautious way he advances from the restrained expression of his body. Notice how he puts only the outside of his right foot on the floor as he steps, indicating being quiet and careful.

Photograph 58   Advancing with slow, careful movement

The second aspect of performance is that the children may be asked, from time to time, to demonstrate how they have responded to the challenges which were set. For example, the teacher might say:

> *Let us all watch Shalom and notice especially how he seems to soar through the air and the soft way he melts into the floor as his dance ends.*

What the teachers say when they ask children to show their dance is of the greatest importance. In this instance, as Shalom listens to the guidelines for viewing which the teacher gives to the class he receives clues about what is expected from his performance. As well as focusing the attention of those watching, it is the teacher's way of reminding him of what he is going to do.

As a result of this his 'thinking body' becomes focused and he is able to give fully of himself. These are two important attributes of performance.

Performing for other people

Sometimes children show their dances to another class, or to the whole school, perhaps at a school assembly or during a time which is set aside for sharing. Occasionally, children show their dance to parents and friends at a special event. When the performance space changes from the hall or class-room to a stage or some other 'theatre space' yet another level of perfor-mance consciousness is reached and a different sort of excitement is felt. When handled well, such occasions are exciting, enriching experiences where children's dance is seen within a supportive and informative setting. Children's dance requires the same serious attention as that given to any other art form in which they express their ideas and feelings. When the 'pro-gramme' represents the children's own work and is seen as an illustration of their artistic and aesthetic development there is little danger of inappropri-ate responses from the audience. It is only when children appear as instru-ments of adult conceptions, as in some Nativity plays where they attempt shepherd's dances and the like, that it can go wrong. The 'ohs', 'ahs' and indulgent and generous smiles of those who watch help to make such per-formances a spectacle. Lowden (1989: 71) expresses a warning:

> consider the kind of sharing that happens, say, at Christmas. At the most limited level of sharing parents come to admire their children and apart from parental pride, the criteria for spectating are those of stage and screen cut down.

The audience needs to know what is involved and how to look in order to understand and respond. Boorman makes a case for the education of parents and 'significant adults' so that they come to know and appreciate their chil-dren in this special kind of setting. She advises:

> We have to ensure that adults recognize that children's art has to be more than mere entertainment; it has to go beyond the 'cute' and become evocation and response between child and adult: a mutual giving and receiving.
>
> (Boorman 1991a)

Writing specifically in relation to children under five years, Stinson (1988: 8) suggests that making a 'show for parents is almost always doomed to failure'. However, as the children progress in their understanding of themselves and of dance this is not necessarily the case and many such performances inform the audience and delight the children. Green Gilbert (1992: 53) makes a strong case against recital type performances while at the same time admits that 'there is little sense in developing skills and learning to express yourself if you never have the opportunity to share these skills with others'. She favours informal showings where the children's knowledge and skills are shared in a variety of contexts: with each other; with parents; with friends.

The child as spectator, appreciator and critic

This part of the three-pronged model has, to some extent, been looked at already. In essence, it is the natural counterpart of performing or showing. Sharing dances with, or performing dances to, friends and peers is a reciprocal process. One minute children are performers, the next minute they are a member – sometimes the only member – of an audience. There surely can be no better way than this of coming to 'know' the art of dance. In the early years of childhood, there is no sense that some can 'do' and others 'only watch', an attitude which, regrettably, sometimes creeps in later on. Because watching is an integral part of the total dance education scenario it has a meaning and a value of its own. And, because the language of dance is a common one, the basis for watching and recognising it is already in place. In examining the relationship between learning through participation in dance and learning about dance, Killingbeck (1993: 4) suggests that:

> *Participation in dance activity makes a unique contribution to a child's aesthetic appreciation of dance as art, and that practical experience fundamentally underpins and is a necessary condition for the development of an aesthetic appreciation of dance as art in education.*

The appreciation element, erroneously thought by some to be missing from dance education of the 1960s and 1970s, has always been central to the learning of young children where *doing and viewing* are considered as interchangeable partners. Children's critical abilities fit naturally into the general practice of early childhood education where looking, listening and commenting have always taken their place as important ingredients of learning. In terms of dance, Bloomfield (2000: 50) considers that children 'develop their critical powers in order to monitor their own performance and that of others'.

Spectating, *viewing* and *appreciating* dance is a progressive affair. Eventually, 'authentic' language is necessary for children, even young children, to fulfil the role. Progression from the two-year-old through to the eight-year-old comes about through the ability to carry out and, more importantly, to relate some of the following spectator activities:

- identifying
- naming
- describing
- commenting upon
- reflecting upon
- critically appraising.

Sometimes spontaneously, and at other times as part of a follow-up experience, children 'talk about' their dances, 'write about' them in terms of a description, a story or a poem or 'draw or paint about' them. This could be considered either as an extension of the dance experience itself or as making a transitory experience more permanent in some form: the children's way of recording.

As part of her research programme to develop a curriculum and teaching strategies for teachers of creative dance for young children, Shu-Ying Liu collaborated with a kindergarten at Hsin-Chu's Science-Based Industrial Park Experimental School in Taiwan. She found that children were encouraged to interpret and extend their learning in dance through critical thinking in other art forms such as drawing and speaking. Their teachers used these 'extension outcomes' to help the children reflect upon their dance experiences and develop their linguistic abilities. Photograph 59, provided by Liu is one of several included in her research. It is called 'Frozen Shapes' and clearly expresses the angularity and articulation of the child's body along with a sharp dynamic as it assumes a variety of held positions.

Dialogue and dance: a shared activity

The first remarks of parents and carers to their children as they dance are important.

- What a lovely stretch your body has.
- You are almost flying through the air.
- That position is really strong.

Photograph 59   Frozen shapes

These are early comments which help to build the foundation on which dance-viewing and the later stage of appreciation are built. They are positive statements resulting from watching the children dance and include movement vocabulary with which the children are familiar. The subsequent succession of people who take on the care and education of young children need to continue to comment in this fashion as they support and enrich the children's dance experience. Questions to the children about their own dances, the dances of their peers and the dances they watch together on the video are important maturation markers. At appropriate times, teachers need to share the responsibility for increasingly informed comment with both individual children and small groups. Around seven and eight years of age that responsibility can be transferred to the children who are gradually able to shape their own critical dialogue. As can be seen from the following extracts, every child will have their own ways both of creating and performing their dances and also of describing them.

The legend of Panku

Children in a class of seven- and eight-year-olds in a primary school in the Midlands are used to making, performing and commenting on their dances. They created and performed a dance based on the legend of Panku. Here is how Suzanne and Gregory, both seven, describe the experience:

Suzanne describes the dance.

> Making our dance
>
> Our dance was based on a Chinese legend. We thought about how Chinese people moved in their long dresses. We did little tiny steps and put our hands together with our elbows out to enter. All our positions were balanced, so we looked calm.
>
> I helped to make up the wind section. We did gentle swirls and turns. We were so soft we did the movement on our own and then joined together to make a cloud that bounced softly and gently in the sky. We turned and turned so gently, then softly creeping we made our way back to our places. I like the movement we made up.

Figure 32   Suzanne describes the dance

Gregory also writes about it (Figure 33).

The different emphasis the children give in their descriptions is interesting. Suzanne calls hers '*Making* our dance', highlighting the process of composition, while Gregory names his '*Performing* the dance', showing his concern for the way in which the dance was carried out. Their comments indicate Suzanne's interest in telling us what the dance was about while Gregory found the element of performance and sharing exciting. Unless the children had articulated their responses to this experience in this way their teacher may not have appreciated their different reactions so comprehensively.

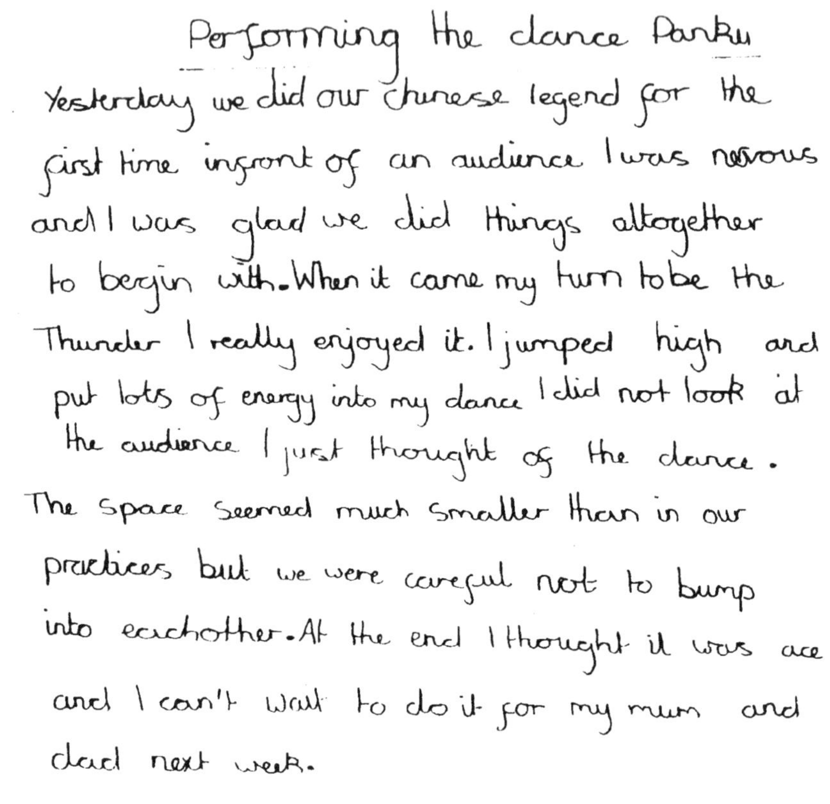

Performing the dance Parku

Yesterday we did our chinese legend for the first time infront of an audience I was nervous and I was glad we did things altogether to begin with. When it came my turn to be the Thunder I really enjoyed it. I jumped high and put lots of energy into my dance I did not look at the audience I just thought of the dance. The space seemed much smaller than in our practices but we were careful not to bump into eachother. At the end I thought it was ace and I can't wait to do it for my mum and dad next week.

Figure 33   Gregory describes the dance

We also learn something of the same dance experience from Photograph 60 showing Timothy, aged seven, who was part of the sun group. He was able to make his body, his costume and the piece of material he handled a meaningful whole as he expressed his ideas of the sun. He moved with confidence and understanding in what for him had become an integrated arts context.

Photograph 60   Timothy's dance

Widening the image of dance

The child's role in viewing dance is helped by contact with the professional world. A very simple and natural way of doing this is through the medium of television and video. Just as children may watch football, rugby, gardening, cookery or house make-over specialists with the rest of the family, so too can they become aware of the professional dancers and dance-makers who increasingly appear on our screens from time to time. These include artists not only from contemporary and classical dance genres but also those from a wide variety of different cultures. The work of educational units, attached to professional companies, has much to offer to children in infant and junior schools. The nature of their involvement varies from company to company but professional dancers are often included in the team that visits the school. Sometimes the visit lasts only half a day but for older children the residency might go on for a week and may be shared with another school. Such a visit or residency can be a rare and exciting treat when children see, and sometimes dance with, 'real dancers' and attend live performances. On these occasions, not only does the children's knowledge of dances and dancers increase but also their thoughts and opinions – their critical powers.

For those children with a special interest in dance

The more young children get interested in things the more they want to do. We looked earlier at children's persistence to conquer traditional skills such as skipping and catching. Thirsts of this kind also apply to the pursuit of favourite categories of interest. Some children have special interests in computers, others in drama, games or poetry. Similarly, some children are 'into dance' and cannot get enough of it. Writing about the development of interests, Katz and Chard (1989: 32) make this point:

> *One of the important dispositions of concern to educators of young children is interest or the capacity to 'lose oneself' in an activity or concern outside oneself.*

Katz goes on to identify the tendency of young children to become:

> *deeply absorbed enough in an activity to pursue it over an extended period of time, with sufficient commitment to accept its routine as well as novel aspects.*

Photograph 61   Marisabel, aged three, from Puerto Rica, enjoys her special dance class

While such enthusiasm is natural enough for children, it often poses problems for parents. This is particularly so in the case of private dance schools where, in addition to payment for classes, there are extra expenses for examinations such as those associated with the Royal Academy of Dance or the Imperial Society of Teachers of Dancing. Should their children enter a situation which as well as being fee paying may be less flexible than they would like, where it involves the acquisition of adult-oriented skills and making a journey? The questions and answers in each case will vary according to philosophy, family priorities and economics, and for some it is the right choice. However, there is now a greater spread of dance opportunities than ever before, including those that allow children to take part in the dance of other cultures such as Asian, Irish and Greek each with its special movement characteristics and style. Costs apart, the question of whether or not young children should be taught set patterns of movement remains debatable. For some it may not be appropriate but for others, who find no stress but only enjoyment in such a situation and gain individual satisfaction within the set parameters, there is perhaps less to fear.

Not all dance opportunities involve great costs. Increasingly, youth dance groups are opening their doors to younger members where the methods of teaching are educationally appropriate, creative workshops a high priority and membership fees low or even non-existent. Saturday clubs provide excellent opportunities and not only cater for young children but also include classes for parents and toddlers. These are in great demand and are well attended. Dance companies, through their education and community units, provide workshops and classes of different kinds as well as introducing children to the dances and dancers of the professional theatre.

Photograph 62   Mothers and toddlers at the South Bank London

Into whatever category dance experience is offered there are huge benefits for the children, especially in view of the restricted availability in the National Curriculum. Importantly, children will be dancing with a group of like-minded enthusiasts; it gives additional scope for the children's dance vocabulary to be widened and for them to be involved in making dances and performing dances with a particular group of people. The children become generally more educated in, about and through dance. The non-dance bonuses for children who participate are equally important. The children gain confidence, build up a sense of belonging, make friends, anticipate and reflect on what is important at any particular time. Such bonuses are not exclusive to dance and, often, children attending dance classes are also members of other activity groups.

Although gaining experience in this way is of value to all children, it is of special significance to those whose intense interest incorporates signs of special ability. We sometimes need reminding that children with an element of 'giftedness' require a measure of special provision just as much as those children with learning difficulties. In a few instances, where a child's interest in dance seems especially strong, the parents may decide that an institution where dance features as a major subject may be a better way of catering for the special interest or potential giftedness of their child than juggling with a traditional school curriculum and after-school dance classes. Again, expense is a consideration although there is an increasing degree of funding available for successful applicants.

Summary

All dance is movement but not all movement is dance. It is the right of all children including those with special educational needs to have access to this important art form. It follows that all early childhood practitioners should do their best to ensure that the dance curriculum, whether in the form of discrete experiences for the very young at the Foundation Stage or the more formalised lessons at Key Stages 1 and 2, has relevance to the wide range of children in their care. Dance has personal and wide connotations. As Gough (1993: Introduction) suggests:

> *Dancing enables us to be comfortable in and with our own bodies. Dance, through its expressive and communicative qualities, allows us to become more conscious of ourselves and the world around us in a unique way.*

8

Dance in statutory education

Good teaching is concerned with more than knowledge, skills and competen-
cies. It is also about an ability to communicate enthusiasm for the subject and
a belief in the right of young people to experience the best possible teaching
environment. It requires from the teacher a continuing curiosity regarding the
process of teaching and learning and an openness to considering ways of
improving the quality of his/her work. (Gough 1993: 27)

Where does dance belong?

Throughout the past two decades debate has increasingly centred on the appropriate 'placing' of dance within the school curriculum. Where does it rightfully belong? Should it be compulsory – a core activity – or should it be optional? There are those who claim that because of the movement basis of dance it belongs, as it has done for many years, as part of the physical education programme. Others, a growing number, argue that it is an art form alongside music, art and drama with which it has strong generic links. In support of this argument Flemming (1973: 5) describes dance as:

> *having the added dimension of aesthetic, creative and inner self expression*
> *which is so important in young children's lives.*

For the time being the long and heated debate has been decided for us – by the government. At the Foundation Stage, specific references to dance are sited in Physical Education (QCA 2000: 103). At the next stage of the National Curriculum dance also appears within the statutory order for Physical Education and takes its place alongside games, gymnastics, swimming, athletics and outdoor activities within the statutory order for physical education (DfEE and QCA 1999: 113).

As long as dance is included somewhere in the curriculum perhaps where it appears matters less for the teaching of young children up to the age of seven years than it does for older children. Arguably, early childhood educators have less in the way of formalised subject categories to restrict them and cross-curricular links emerge naturally for children and adults alike. In making a case for an interrelated curriculum mode Bloomfield (2000: 1) argues that:

> *the integrated arts mode accords dance, drama, music and visual art a collective, central and pivotal role in primary education.*

Interpreting guidelines and attaining targets

In relation to effective learning at the Foundation Stage the guidelines propose:

* offering a range of stimuli for movement, such as action rhymes, stories, music and props
* introducing the vocabulary of movement and words of instruction.

Subsequent pages of the document suggest 'stepping stones' with examples of what the children do and what the practitioners 'need to do'. It is unfortunate that the format of the latter section appears to encourage prescription as some of the stepping stones are worthy of more in-depth exploration and implementation. There are, however, some helpful hints to be found in the following section on Creativity, concerned with providing children with opportunities to develop their own ideas.

In Key Stage 1 the programme of study for Physical Education (Dance) requires that pupils should be taught to:

* use movement imaginatively, responding to stimuli including music, and performing basic skills (for example, travelling, being still, making a shape, jumping, turning and gesturing)
* change the rhythm, speed, level and direction of their movements
* create and perform dances using simple movement patterns, including those from different times and cultures
* express and communicate ideas and feelings.

At Key Stage 2 the programme of study indicates that pupils should be taught to:

- create and perform dances using a range of movement patterns including those from different times, places and cultures
- respond to a range of stimuli and accompaniment.

Specific units that flesh out these brief and general guidelines for dance activities are published by the QCA and DfEE (2000). They give important information which tells us:

- about the unit (*in general terms*)
- where it fits in (*to the general scheme*)
- vocabulary (*the range of words and phrases the children might use*)
- resources (*for example, cassette player, percussion*)
- expectations (*the sorts of outcomes teachers could expect*).

The unit goes on to provide further detail in tabulating learning objectives, possible teaching activities and learning outcomes.

Theory into practice

Where do we go from here?

From this generalised departure point it becomes the responsibility of the teacher to decipher information and to make it accessible to the children in the form of lessons and schemes of work. The question is, how can this be achieved? Due to the reappraisal of National Curriculum priorities there is now a vast difference in the amount of time spent and depth reached between Dance and the core subjects of English, Mathematics and Science in the initial training of teachers. This difference is also reflected in the small amount of time for teachers already in post to participate in courses and conferences related to Dance in education. Although some manage to include attendance at national and regional courses run by the National Dance Teachers Association (NDTA) and local authorities, for them too the focus of their in-service training is predominantly on the core curriculum.

As a result teachers in the Foundation Stage and at Key Stages 1 and 2 are especially appreciative of the small stream of literature which assists them in the preparation and implementation of the dance curriculum. There is no doubt that such material is helpful. This is particularly so where teachers are made aware of the principles behind the practical suggestions and can go on from exemplars to create suitable lesson material of their own

(Bloomfield 2000, Gough 1993, Peter 1997, Rolfe and Harlow 1992). However, where the literature consists of a series of set lessons there are clearly inherent difficulties for long-term use. Where such lessons appear as ends in themselves the dangers are clear. Dance lessons unrelated to the children's particular interests, developmental sequences and their peers with whom they work may be ineffective or restrictive. For the teachers, the continuous repetition of material can result in boring, non-reflective and uninformed practice.

This chapter attempts to accompany and endorse the good practice of colleagues who have successfully matched principles and practice. The suggestions for the lessons which are given as samples or exemplars use the theoretical underpinning which characterises the preceding chapters of the book and include:

- an appropriate and detailed movement vocabulary which is a major ingredient of dance and which is basically featured in the guidelines of the Foundation Stage and Key Stages 1 and 2 of the National Curriculum
- the concept of the child as creator, performer and appreciator
- physical, cognitive and social development which has implications for the setting and progression of work
- ways in which dance fits into education of children under five years and sets the scene for Key Stages 1 and 2
- attention given to key learning phases
- the importance and use of observation techniques
- expressive movement.

Mix and match

As indicated in Chapter 7, taking into account developmental sequencing, prior experience, length of time and available resources, many of the ideas and themes can be used appropriately with a variety of age settings and contexts. The following examples feature work in the Foundation Stage as well as at Key Stages 1 and 2. In no way are these templates or lessons set in stone. Of course in the short term they are there to be used, to be tried and tested. However, the hope is that teachers will consider the educational and movement principles underpinning the lessons as ingredients for them, and through them their children, to mix, match and make as appropriate. To emphasise this I have deliberately avoided using an exact structure or identical language for all the lessons. The Foundation Stage begins with a section that suggests ways in which simple ideas can be used spontaneously during the day and which concentrates on the sharing relationship of children and their teachers and carers. In the two more structured sessions which follow I have used personalised comments illustrating what the teacher might actually say. At other times suggestions and comments are made in an impersonalised way. In some instances follow-up lessons are suggested while, in others, snippets only are indicated. To *Look and listen* is juxtaposed with alternatives to *See and say* and *Observe and discuss*. The selection is used in association with the developmental context in which they occur.

Preparation and reflection

Rather than cluttering the lesson plans with too many teaching strategies Foundation Stage lessons are *preceded* by an introductory discussion of salient points. At Key Stages 1 and 2 a discussion *follows* the lessons identifying a rationale and critical appraisal of what has been proposed. In this way an attempt has been made to pursue the main thread of this book that theory should inform effective practice.

> *The dance lesson like any other teaching must have a sense of purpose, but only the teacher can really identify the point of the lesson.* (Lowden 1989: 81)

The reference to 'Challenges' in the lesson structure may seem rather prescriptive and out of place in a book on early childhood education. However the term (which is not sacrosanct and can be replaced with any of the teacher's choice) is used precisely because it reflects the development of thinking pertinent to all children from birth to eight years – and beyond. It relates to the phases of learning identified in Chapter 5 and especially to Vygotsky's ideas of children operating where they happen to be in their spectrum of endeavour and where, with the help of the teacher or 'significant others', to go that bit further. A 'challenge' whichever way you look at it.

Common to all the children's dance experiences is the place and importance of evaluation. Reflection on 'how things went' is one of several short- and long-term monitoring and review procedures. In respect of all the exemplar lessons that follow, an important element of teaching dance is to reflect upon what has taken place and, in the light of this, to decide what to do next. The possibilities are endless and necessarily always relate to a particular situation and group of children. They include but are not restricted to:

- repeating the entire structure of the previous lesson
- keeping the structure but adding/changing accompaniment
- making the challenges greater – increasing the struggle, deepening the experience
- deciding to take a different idea
- considering the children's current interests and using them as a resource
- making links with other areas of the curriculum.

The Foundation Stage

Although the learning environment along with the organisation and structure of the day will be different there is very little which distinguishes children themselves on the day they start statutory schooling and the day before. Gradually, adaptation will come about and the prime aims and objectives of infant-oriented and later junior-oriented education will begin to be realised. However, in Dance, as in other aspects of the curriculum, the last year of the Foundation Stage and the first year of Key Stage 1 are in some instances almost interchangeable. Certainly the line between them is very faint: it is often a matter of balance, emphasis and expectation. It is perhaps therefore helpful for those involved at both 'stages' (the official wording not mine) to anticipate and reflect upon what happens 'before' 'during' and 'after' transition times in order to make them as seamless as possible.

Making it up as we go along

The dance experience of three- and four-year-olds often begins with a child dancing in a space, observed by the teacher who seizes on the 'happening' and builds on it. It may be sufficient for the teacher to say to the children *who happen to be around at the time* something like:

> *Look at Eddie dancing round the room in all those different ways. I have some music here. Let's all join in.*

That may be it – the sum total of the dance experience. It is important that the taking up of the idea is immediate and spontaneous otherwise the moment will be lost. The teacher needs to have some music ready to play or to let the dancing happen without any accompaniment.

On other occasions the starting point may be 'held in the teacher's mind' ready to be put to use at an appropriate moment, just as a book may be taken from a shelf when the need is identified. Such 'starters' may have their origins in an action rhyme or a story such as the *bean stalk growing taller and taller*. Schema-sharing is also a good stimulus for dancing together and does not need to wait until the children are older. For example, identifying bodily structure through the children exploring the use of parts of their own bodies, a skeleton or a puppet on a string, has endless possibilities.

Ideas involving the participation of early childhood practitioners usually bring about interesting dance experiences. *I move and you move* is one where the teacher dances and the children are still and then the children dance while the teacher is still. Taking it in turns is a simple compositional aid and demands the attention of the children as they experience stillness and action – waiting to go and having to stop.

Teacher in the middle is another relationship experience. The teacher stands in the centre of the space and the children around the edges. They are encouraged to move very slowly towards her but not to touch her. When the last child arrives the teacher claps her hands or spins around (or carries out any dance action he/she chooses) and the children dance away leaving him/her alone again. Children delight in dance play interaction of this sort. It is then up to the children and the teacher to concoct varieties of dancing based on this theme of *near and far* often *making it up as they go along*.

Green Gilbert (1992: 17) suggests:

> *It is very difficult to teach dance to children under the age of two without parents, because young children need to be carried and manipulated most of the time.*

It *is* difficult if this is taken to mean groups of children. But there are lots of occasions during the day when toddlers can dance with one of the adults in their play areas as they do with members of their families at home. Of special interest here is Photograph 62 (Chapter 7) which features a mother dancing with her two children. With one on her back and the other dancing in front of her it shows a wonderfully cohesive relationship.

If children at the Foundation Stage have had lots of opportunities to dance and prance at will and have experienced dancing in the company of others, if provision in terms of materials, music and space are freely available and dancing is established as a familiar activity in the daily provision then they will be well prepared and eager to enter into simply structured dance 'sessions' such as the two which follow here.

Introducing a blowing bubbles dance

This is a fun dance. It incorporates all three categories of the child as creator, performer and spectator, with an emphasis on the two last roles. Basically it involves an exaggeration of breathing – blowing – and the sense of touch. It grows naturally from blowing bubbles, an activity that the children are likely to have experienced in their early childhood. However, it will add to the meaning of the dance for them to 're-experience' hence the inclusion of bubble blowing as a suggested prerequisite.

Because of its potential complexities readers may wonder why this lesson is included in the Foundation Stage section. Why not at Key Stage 1 or even Key Stage 2? The reasoning here is that the dance experiences can be kept to a minimum especially with the very young children, perhaps just using the first challenge ending with the section 'See and say'. This snippet can be repeated on several occasions including in response to requests 'Can we do our bubble dance today?' Sessions for the four-year-olds, many of whom will be in Reception classes, could focus on Challenge 2 which invites more detailed movement exploration and expression while the five-year-olds, in whatever setting, will probably be able to manage both these challenges within one lesson.

At Key Stage 1 the first four challenges are likely to be within the children's comprehension while by Key Stage 2 the seven- and eight-year-olds should be able to cope with the final task of creating their own dances to music. Most children at this age will be able to retain the previous different dance experiences, select those they most enjoy and make them into a finished personal dance which they can repeat and discuss. An excellent example of three girls creating a dance and talking about it with an adult is shown in the NDTA video (1998: 13:49).

Throughout these six different but related sections of the dance lesson the teacher is deeply involved in setting appropriate child-related challenges, observing responses and helping the children to comment. These teaching roles are interrelated and for all three it is important to have some idea of the movement ideas which will be used. These are listed at the start of the lesson/session plan and have been selected from the theoretical framework in Chapter 1:

- gentle, floating movement from the area of dynamics – *how the children move*
- use of hands from the body section – *what the children move*
- articulation of body parts from the body section – *what the children move*
- making patterns in the air from the space section – *where the children move*
- use of levels from the space section – *where the children move.*

The same theme of blowing bubbles can be envisaged and planned in a variety of ways and a different selection of movement ideas selected. The common denominator is that in the development of both dance and spoken language the observations to be made and the questions asked of the children must relate to what they have done. This start in critical appraisal is an important one.

Blowing bubbles dance

Resources	Free uncluttered space (either indoors or outside).
Dance idea	Bubbles.
Pre-experience	Blowing bubbles (either earlier in the day or at the start of the lesson).
Movement ideas	• gentle, floating movement
	• use of hands
	• articulation of different body parts
	• making patterns in the air
	• use of levels
	• working within a general framework of music.
Challenge 1	Children to move freely expressing their own ideas about bubbles and their movement.
Learning phase	Free exploration.
See and say	Teacher selects two or three children to show their dancing and asks the rest of the children what they noticed about the dancing of the children they were watching.
Challenge 2	Children to experiment with the following:
	• blowing bubble from one hand into the air and catching it on the other hand encouraging gentle, careful movement

> - blowing bubbles from one hand and catching them on another part of the body, e.g. back, shoulder, knee.

Learning phase	Guided exploration.
Teacher's role	To observe children as they move and to make ongoing general and individual commentaries on the different parts of the body being used to catch the bubbles.
Challenge 3	Children to make up blowing bubbles dance where, in turn, they blow three bubbles and make them land on three different parts of the body.
Learning phase	Guided exploration (leading to creation).
Teacher's role	To make general comments relating to the quality of movement being expressed and bodily 'landing pads'.
See and say	Children observe each other and comment on the use of the body parts being used for the bubble to land.
Challenge 4	Blowing bubbles with more energy and following them as they float through the air and land on the ground.
Learning phase	Guided exploration.
Teacher's role	To encourage the children to make patterns in the air as they follow their bubbles' 'space journey'.
Challenge 5	Making a bubble dance.
Learning phase	Consolidation (leading to creation).
Teacher's role	To help children to set a structure:

> - blow a bubble and catch it on one body part
> - blow a bubble and catch on a different body part
> - blow a bubble and follow its pattern until it lands on the floor.

Challenge 6	Children to create their own bubble dances to music.
Learning phase	Free exploration (leading to creation).

An introduction to the punching and jumping dances

These two dance lessons, presented as successive sessions need not be taken in this form. The first lesson need not be followed by lesson 2 and neither does it need to be taken in its entirety. This is partly what was implied earlier when it was suggested that material can be used in different ways with different sets of children. For the three-year-olds *either* a rather more 'global' punching *or* jumping dance experience may be sufficient. For the four- and five-year-olds a session/lesson might include both experiences.

The emphasis at different times within the two lessons incorporates notions of the children as *creators* and *performers*. It is important that teachers should have in mind what strategies will bring this creative and performance emphasis into being. In terms of the children creating their dances several compositional factors are included in the first of the two lessons the main one being *linking* (see Chapter 7). On this occasion the compositional element of linking is brought about by:

- the establishment of two 'child-owned' spaces in the room
- the second part of the dance being preceded by stillness
- the introduction of sound for the second part of the dance.

In terms of *the performance element* it is essential to return time and time again to the movement vocabulary of the children and to consider ways to both extend and deepen their perception of how the body is used. The NDTA (1998: 10) reminds us that 'central to developing pupils' skills, knowledge and understanding in creating, performing and appreciating dances is an understanding of movement itself'.

In both lessons 1 and 2 the teacher clearly has three aspects in mind in the exploratory punching activities. These are:

- the articulation of different parts of hands and arms
- using the space around the body
- the quality of strength.

Having chosen this appropriate selection of categories it is essential to know how to help the children. For example, in using the space around the body, *zones and directions* need to be actively explored; *surfaces and joints* are important in the articulation of arms and hands, while *strength* involves help about maintaining a wide base, gripping the muscles and not letting the punching go too far away from the body thus losing the strength. In providing help it is important to remember that movement experiences can be taken out of the context of a particular lesson; children can be given discrete experiences in the bodily, spatial or qualitative spheres in order to enhance meaning before returning to the lesson theme in question.

A punching and jumping dance (1)

Stimulus/theme	Punching and jumping actions.
Challenge 1	Run about the room punching the air as you go.
Learning phase	Guided exploration initiated by the teacher.
Challenge 2	This time stay in one place and find some different ways of punching the space around you.
Teacher's role	To encourage the following movement responses as a start to *creating* a punching dance:

- keeping on the spot punch the space around your body
- use different parts of your hands and arms to punch
- how about the elbows? Try punching with them
- make your movement as strong as possible.

Challenge 3	This time try out some jumping ideas as you move around the room.
Learning phase	Guided exploration initiated by the teacher.
Teacher's role	To encourage the following movement responses as an aid to *creating* a jumping dance:

- look where you are now and run to another place in the room
- look back, see where you came from and run back to that place
- this time jump all the way to your new place
- and back again
- try to do more than just one kind of jump this time – I am going to look for children doing two kinds of jumps.

Looking and talking	Look at A and B's jumping dance. What sort of jumps are they doing?
Learning phase	Consolidation and extension.
Challenge 3	Try your jumping dance again going from your first place to your second place. Give your dance a special ending and be very still.
Looking and talking	Teacher comments on some of the special endings and encourages all the children to have one last try.

A punching and jumping dance (2)

Stimulus/theme	Punching and jumping actions.
Challenge 1	Recapping jumping dances.
Learning phase	Consolidation.
Teacher's role	To help the children remember the structure of their jumping dances especially:

- moving from one place in the room to another
- concentrating on two jumps
- holding a still position at the end.

Challenge 2	Revisiting the punching dances introduced at the start of the previous lesson and reiterating their ideas.
Learning phase	Consolidation.
Teacher's role	To enhance the *performance* element in:

- punching the space around your body
- the use of different parts of your hands and arms
- making your movement as strong as possible
- making a special ending to your punching dance.

Challenge 3	Dance your punching dance and when you hear the drum being played change to your jumping dance.
Looking and talking	Look at two children carrying out their punching and jumping dance and discuss such successful elements as:

- strong punching
- effective changeover
- still endings
- varied jumping.

Learning phase	Everyone has another go.

Key Stage 1

Our winter dances

Dance idea	Action words and phrases.
Teacher's role	To ask the children to listen to the following action words.

> *Shivering, shivering, freeze*
> *shivering, shivering, freeze*
> *drip, drip, and melt right away.*

Challenge 1	To move as the words are spoken.

Learning phase	Free exploration.
Teacher's role	To look at the children moving and to make some comments en route to help them produce the maximum expression of their bodies during this period of improvisation.
Challenge 2	To take the first two shivering phrases and make them into a repeatable pattern.
Learning phase	Guided exploration (leading to creation).
Teacher's role	To help the children gain clarity of expression through movement-oriented comments such as:

- make the shivering sometimes happen in one bit of you and at other times go all through your body
- make the freeze a sudden, sharp movement
- make your shape really jagged and spiky
- hold the freeze shape very still.

Challenge 3	After the teacher has reiterated the four 'remember points' the children are asked to do their shivering phrases again.
Learning phase	Consolidation and extension (in-depth understanding).
Look and listen	Half of the class shows their phrases to the other half who are asked to look out for individuals who had managed to achieve some of the things asked for and to say why they had been selected. Groups change over dancing and observer roles.
Challenge 4	To improvise the second action phrase of:

> *Drip, drip and melt right away.*

Learning phase	Free exploration.
Teacher's role	To ask children to:

- suggest and discuss some words to describe their dripping and melting right away
- experiment making short dripping movement from more unusual parts of the body, e.g. elbows, knees, heads
- make melting movements as slow as possible until all parts of their bodies are on the ground.

Learning phase	Guided exploration.
Challenge 5	Create a winter dance to the whole phrase:

> *Shivering, shivering, freeze*
> *shivering, shivering, freeze*
> *drip, drip, and melt right away.*

Look and listen
- children to watch and dance in two groups. To select and comment on dances that interest them and that show the special aspects upon which they had been working.
- children asked for one thing that could be done to improve any of the dances they had seen and discussed.

Challenge 6   Children to dance their dances as well as they can this time saying the words themselves as an accompaniment.

Our winter dances: rationale, review and reflections

This dance is primarily featured for children who are in the first two years of statutory schooling, although a simpler and more selective use may be used with younger children. The stimulus is the use of action words spoken by the teacher in the first instance and then by the children. The lesson is written from the teacher's perspective.

Taken in its entirety, it can be seen that attention is given to the creating, performing and appreciating roles of the children as they dance, observe and talk together. One significant progression at Key Stage 1 is the expectation that the children can relate their comments more closely to the facilitating guidelines set by the teacher. As well as being asked to comment upon what they see as successful outcomes they are encouraged to suggest *one thing* that might make a particular dance even better. This engenders fostering a sense of priority in their critical appraisal.

Within this lesson a short section is allocated to the children's suggestions and discussion of some of the action words being used. An alternative way of using action words is by taking language as a starting point. Williams (1991: 29), using a similar action phrase of *shaking, shivering and shuddering* explained how 'dance was explored as one way to promote understanding and shared meaning of a particular classroom topic'. She stresses that the action phrase was chosen as an accompaniment *after* activity work in the classroom and from words that had been used by both children and teacher. In the classroom the children had been working on the topic of *water* where activities included making ice and watching it melt; filling egg cups with water from a dripping tap; and hanging the wet mopping up cloth outside during a frosty morning. The following differentiation between the three words, which can be identified within the movement framework in Chapter 1, is quoted here in its entirety:

Mark   Shaking is sort of *bigger and all over* Miss.
Jenny   Shivering is when *bits of you* go – *kind of shaking but littler* –
              like when just your teeth *chatter* or your tummy.

Some children made trips outside to see that the damp cloth was gradually
stiffening and commented:

Adnam   Its going all crunchy.
Mark   You can see all the cracks and creases in it.
Ben   When it was wet it was just a soft heap, now its on the desk
              and it sort of rocks on the pointy bits.

In class, a cube of ice had been placed on the desk and allowed to melt. Here
the comments were:

Paula   The edges is getting smoother.
Michelle   Its growing a puddle.
James   And its so slow you can hardly see it happening.
Clive   Its going to spread all over the desk.
Adrian   All that big flat curvy shape from one little square.

Williams (1991: 31) concludes that:

> *each encounter should be illuminated by appraisals from many previous
> encounters in a range of different situations. The dance lesson can be used as
> one of those different situations, as an ideal opportunity for fostering specific
> language skills in individual children and if these opportunities can include
> dialogue based on previous classroom discussion then these lessons can
> contribute to children's skills of understanding and communicating.*

Cymbal Dance

Stimulus/theme   Movement and sound partners.
Sound ideas   Arising from the use of a cymbal and beater played by the
                     teacher.
Movement ideas   Body:
                     • shape
                     • stretching and collapsing.

Dynamics:
- suddenness
- slow and lingering
- light and gentle.

Space:
- levels
- on the spot and travelling
- high and low.

Listen and comment	Children asked to listen to the sound of the ringing cymbal and to describe the sort of sound it made and the number of times the sound happened.
Challenge 1	Children asked to travel and settle to each phrase of the cymbal.
Learning phase	Guided exploration (leading to creation).
Teacher's role	To observe the qualities and descriptions provided by the children (likely to include the movement ideas above). To select three or four children to show their movement to the rest of the children asking them to comment on: • the words which described how they moved • the pathways they took while travelling • the body shape they held at the end of each phrase.
Challenge 2	Children to practise travelling making curving, twisting patterns in the air.
Learning phase	Free exploration.
Teacher's role	Making general and individual comments as children move in order to enhance *performance qualities.*
Challenge 3	To move again to the three phrases of the cymbal.
Learning phase	Consolidation.
Listen and comment	Children asked to listen to the following rhythm being played on the cymbal consisting of six taps on the rim of the cymbal followed by one strong beat that gradually fades away.
Challenge 4	As they sit and listen children asked to breathe in and stretch up as the series of tapping sounds is played and then suddenly exhale as the strong ringing sound is heard.
Learning phase	Guided exploration.
Challenge 5	To find a space in the room and take up a shape near the ground – perhaps a new shape or one they used earlier in

the lesson.

To stretch up slowly to the tapping rhythm and hold a new high-up shape and to crumble or collapse as the final sound occurs.

Teacher's role	To add appropriate verbal encouragement in addition to playing the cymbal (not an easy task!) and to let the children dance the phrase several times.
Learning phase	Guided exploration (leading to creation and consolidation).
Listen and comment	Children asked to listen to the two different ways in which the cymbal had been played and to discuss some of the same and different things they had done.
Challenge 6	Children try out dancing the first phase followed by the second phase.

Cymbal dance: rationale, review and reflections

In providing sound accompaniment the teacher has to make yet another significant contribution to the lesson. In situations such as this the children's responses are dependent upon both the compositional aspects of the phrases the teacher creates and the sensitive playing of the instrument. It takes considerable preparation time to:

- select a really good quality instrument
- produce the right sort of sound
- maintain consistency in repeating the phrases
- talk occasionally while it is happening.

It is rather like not only tapping your head and rubbing your tummy, but also bending your knees at the same time! Therefore, in the case of teachers who have no previous experience and would like to try using percussion as a stimulus or accompaniment, it may need some time to experiment before taking the class! It is a mammoth task but one worthwhile in introducing sound in this way: it links well with the music curriculum and is a forerunner of times when children can dance and play percussion instruments themselves.

This is a lengthy dance experience consisting of six different 'challenges'. It can be divided into two or three sessions and the ratio of deepening the movement vocabulary increased as more time is spent on each session. It is helpful to have some movement ideas in mind but, dependent on the children's movement and verbal responses, on-the-spot changes and modifications may need to be made. Similarly, individual teachers will have different sets of movement ideas upon which they want to concentrate, different things upon which to focus according to the previous experiences of the children. The movement ideas listed at the start of the lesson plan therefore reflect personal choices for the teaching of this particular lesson.

Readers will notice that because of the partnering of sound and movement there is more emphasis on listening and commenting than on watching. Only once are some children asked to show their dances. Another thing to notice is that in Challenge 2 the teacher has taken part of the dance phrase out of context. The theme is momentarily left while the teacher's concentration is directed towards improving the children's movement vocabulary. This is an important input because a continually increasing vocabulary is needed in order to express ideas more relevantly and extensively.

There is rather a sense of unfinished business at the end of this lesson. This is intentional. It poses the question of what, if anything, could or should be done next. The theme could be continued in a variety of different ways, for example, some children dancing the first phrase and others the second phrase; it could be developed into partner or small group dances or put into a musical framework. There are so many possibilities.

Key Stage 2

Firework dances

Stimulus   Fireworks.
Movement ideas   Related to choice of fireworks made by the children. These
                      are likely to include:
                      Body:
                      ● actions
                      ● articulation of body parts
                      ● design.
                      Dynamics:
                      ● suddenness
                      ● lingering
                      ● light and gentle
                      ● strong and powerful.

	Space:
	● levels
	● direction
	● pathways and patterns.
Accompaniment	Children's vocal sounds and body percussion.
Challenge 1	To try out moving 'like' two fireworks of their choice.
	To choose fireworks that are very different.
Learning phase	Guided exploration (improvisation).
Teacher's role	Observes and comments to class and individual children helping them to clarify what they are trying to express.
Observe and discuss	Children discuss some of the fireworks being shown, e.g.:
	● those with straight pathways and those with circular pathways
	● those with a 'spluttery', irregular action
	● those with a steady continuous action which gradually slows down.
Challenge 2	Children asked to choose one of the fireworks they have been working on and this time concentrate on three stages of display:
	● the ignition – how it starts to work
	● the main action – the way the body moves
	the dynamics
	the levels, pathways and patterns
	● the way the firework ends
	the fade out
	the explosion.
Learning phase	Consolidation (leading to enhanced role of children as creators).
Teacher's role	Observe the children and identify some of the help that several children needed – perhaps to work on the following:
	● directions
	● pathways in the air and along the floor
	● different dynamic qualities.
Challenge 3	Children to have another attempt at dancing their fireworks.
Learning phase	Consolidation (enhanced understanding and expression).
Teacher's role	At appropriate intervals to stop the class and remind them, e.g.:
	● when ignited to enliven the body and be prepared to go into action

	• to make sure the ending is clear.
Observe and discuss	Children divided into two groups – the performers and the critics. Critics are asked to watch and comment on: • those who showed the three phases clearly • those whose fireworks were clearly patterned • those who performed with expressive dynamics. Critics and performers change over.
Challenge 4	To accompany their dances with voice sounds or sounds from using the body, e.g. accentuating foot patterns, using body percussion.
Learning phase	Extension (involving relating dance and sound).
Challenge 5	To create a firework duet through the following means:
Teacher's role	To guide the children to find a partner who has chosen a different firework to dance: • number 1 dances his/her firework dance and finishes near his/her partner. • as if the last spark had set it alight number 2 dances his/her firework.
Learning phase	Extension (involving partner work).
Teacher's role	Teacher observes, gives individual help and at appropriate times makes suggestions such as: • the first dancer to start away from partner only landing near partner at very end of the dance • no gap between one firework ending and the next one starting.
Challenge 6	Children to change over.

Firework dances: rationale, review and reflections

Although the nature and purpose of their use may vary in different countries, cultures and occasions, the use of fireworks is an international occurrence. The 'show' in which fireworks are let off can range from a few carefully hand-held sparklers in the garden to multi-million displays such as those which greeted the millennium. Fireworks are a seasonal or festivity landmark for many children, a landmark associated with an excitement that cannot easily be ignored. As a result in many countries they have become a favourite theme for dance lessons.

In Chapter 7 a variety of sources for dance was identified including those from the natural and human-made environment. The fireworks dance is an example from this category and was selected partly because of its particular relevance to compositional stages of dance-making. The lesson was structured for children of about seven and eight years of age implying that they are able to handle dance vocabulary, vocal sounds, body percussion and relate to partners or small groups. This is a tough set of challenges. However, as the lesson plan shows, there is a gradual structural build-up to the way in which all these abilities appear, interrelate and develop. The teacher's role in this development is a crucial part of the learning environment. The movement ideas are those with which my colleagues, students and I have experimented. In this sense they have been tried and tested. However, they represent only a few of many possible selections. The compositional structure arises and is developed from the three-phase nature of fireworks namely the ignition, the main action and the ending. At this age, either through participation or as spectators, children will be aware of these various stages but, as in the case of the bubble dances, dances about fireworks are best linked to seasonal activities and immediate experience.

The lesson plan finishes with the concept of partner dances helped by the linking process previously identified with creating individual work. However, that need not be the end. Partner ideas could be extended to the creation of small group dances or a lesson could even begin with group dances. It all depends on the children's previous experience, the teacher's previous experience, links with other areas of the curriculum and seizing opportunities of the moment such as a birthday celebration.

Anything you can do I can do better

Stimulus	Children's love of competing with themselves and others.
Accompaniment	Schwanda the Bagpiper by Weinberg.
	A piece of music with eight 8 bar phrases.
Movement ideas	Body:
	• actions.
	Relationships:
	• alone
	• trio.
Challenge 1	To improvise to music.
Learning phase	Free exploration.

Teacher's role	To look out for a variety of dance activities taking place and to be used in the next part of the lesson.
Observing and identifying	Children using:

- different ways of *jumping*
- different *steps*
- different *gestures.*

Challenge 2	To make up a sequence of steps, gestures and jumps making sure there is a definite starting point, sequence of events and an ending.
Learning phase	Guided exploration (leading to creation).
Teacher's role	To encourage individuality of dancing through the following guidelines as appropriate:

- include different length of the three actions
- start in the same place in the room each time, take the same route to your finishing place
- pay attention to transitions between the three actions
- notice two people near to you at the end.

Challenge 3	To work in one place alongside the two children nearest them trying out some energetic, agile or acrobatic activities. To decide upon one activity they all enjoy doing.
Learning phase	Guided exploration.
Teacher's role	To travel round the room making sure that trios have been established and are able to answer the set task.
Looking and commenting	Children to look at several trios and note the type of activity being danced.
Challenge 4	Using music phrases 5, 6, 7 and 8 children asked to work out a competitive sequence. **NB For purposes of this lesson jumping is the activity** *Dancer 1* dances his/her jumping sequence (phrase 5). *Dancer 2* takes Dancer 1's sequence and tries to make it more complex, difficult, exciting (phrase 6). *Dancer 3* tries to complicate the original sequence even more or dance it in a different way (phrase 7). *All three dancers* dance their own version with energy and precision (phrase 8).
Learning phase	Guided exploration (leading to group dance-making).
Teacher's role	To help individual groups and at appropriate intervals make the following suggestions:

- make clear the nature of the complication, e.g. is the jumping speeded up, does it include turning, achieve greater height?
- find a way of participating while the others are dancing
- make the dance build to a climax at the end when all three are doing their version as best they can to 'outshine' the others.

Challenge 5 To put together the two sections of the dance:
- to start in own space and travel to meet up as a trio
- to make a transition into the trio dance.

Learning phase Extension.

Observe and With the aim to:
discuss
- select successful dances and give reasons why
- give improvement hints explaining their purpose.

Teacher's role To play the music while the children listen.
To ask the children to 'think inside' their dances.
To remind the children of the theme of the dance.

Challenge 6 To dance the dances right through this time concentrating on performing as well as they can.

Anything you can do I can do better: rationale, review and reflection

Children of this age love to compete both with themselves and with their friends. This dance fosters a fun way of entering a competing situation. There are, of course, no winners or losers. The competitive element is lodged in the ability to do something unusual, more exciting, more complex while building on what has gone before. In Vygotsky's terms it could be said that the children's concentration is on taking the next achievement step both in terms of creating and performing.

The music, Schwanda the Bagpiper, is an excellent stimulus and accompaniment for this dance. It is accessible in its phrasing, is quick and vital in mood and increases in momentum in accordance with the growing frenzy of the movement. It is fairly short and 'singable'. There are lots of other pieces with similar characteristics which are there for the listening!

This dance situation is demanding in that the trio relies a great deal on the discussion and structuring of the dance by the children themselves. At about eight years of age children are able to see things from other people's points of view and they can manage the give and take of ideas as required here. They will enjoy the challenge, although verbal exchange may get a bit noisy and the teacher needs to be especially active in spotting needs and giving help.

In their role of appreciators as they watch the responses of their peers their critical abilities are seen as more detailed and reasoned. They can give reasons for success and helpful suggestions to make things better. In preparation for their performance they are able to mentally rehearse the dance while the music is played, especially when the teacher reminds them of the theme of the dance.

Summary – or starting point

Dance as experienced by young children as makers, doers and spectators necessarily has some things in common with professional dance but it needs to be understood and conducted in relation to a sound educational framework.

Bringing it full circle, and connecting the world of the child with the world of professional dance, Judith Jamison, an American contemporary dancer, comments:

> *There's only one of me. There's only one of anybody. That's why different steps look different on different people.*

9

Conclusion

Movement matters. Most adults know this and make great efforts to support their children in the activities of their choice. We are on the way to a stage where movement is accepted as an essential part of early childhood education in its own right and regarded as a respectable and respected contribution to the learning process of young children. But we are only just on the way and what is needed now is consideration of three things.

The first is for early childhood practitioners to do everything they can to ensure that movement and dance become equal partners with other activities in the teaching learning environment. Secondly, for movement and dance practitioners worldwide to share their practice, the observations they make and the records they keep of children's learning in and through a movement perspective with their early childhood partners. And, thirdly, for researchers and theorists to use the work of the practitioners as they continue to look into the principles upon which good practice in early childhood education and care is based. When this dialogue occurs on a regular and systematic basis, movement and dance will most certainly take their rightful place within an early childhood context and movement will be 'seen to matter'.

Bibliography

A Puffin Quartet of Poets (1958) E. Graham (ed.). Harmondsworth: Penguin Books.

Allen, R., Lilley, T. and G. Smith (2000) 'Creative expression', in R. Drury, L. Miller and R. Campbell (eds), *Looking at Early Years Education and Care.* London: David Fulton.

Arnold, P.J. (1988) *Education, Movement and the Curriculum.* London: The Falmer Press.

Athey, C. (1990) *Extending Thought in Young Children: A Parent–Teacher Partnership.* London: Paul Chapman Publishing.

Ball, C. (1994) *Start Right: The Importance of Early Learning.* London: RSA.

Bartenieff, I. with Lewis, D. (1980) *Body Movement: Coping With the Environment.* New York: Gordon and Breach Science.

Bartholomew, L. and Bruce, T. (1993) *Getting To Know You: A Guide to Record-keeping in Early Childhood Education and Care.* London: Hodder and Stoughton.

Bissex, G. (1980) *A Child Learns to Write and Read.* Cambridge MA: Harvard University Press.

Blakemore, C. (1998) 'Experiments worth repeating'. *Nursery World*, 24 September.

Blakemore, S.J. (2000) *POST Report Early Years Education.* London: The Parliamentary Office of Science and Technology.

Bloomfield, A. with Childs, J. (2000) *Teaching Integrated Arts in the Primary School.* London: David Fulton.

Boorman, J. (1969) *Creative Dance in the First Three Grades.* Canada: Longmans Canada.

Boorman, J. (1991a) 'The right and wrong curtsey', Sheila Stanley Memorial Address. Canada.

Boorman, J. (1991b) 'She's just pulled the blanket over her face: the essential role of the creative arts in early childhood', in L. Young Overby (ed.), *Early*

Childhood Creative Arts. American Alliance for Health, Physical Education, Recreation and Dance, pp. 14–25.

Boorman, J. (1991c) *The Colour Goblins and the Golden Cradle: music, language and dance for children four to eight years*. Edmonton: University of Alberta Publication Services.

Boorman, P. (1987) 'The contributions of physical activity to development in the early years', in G. Blenkin and V. Kelly (eds), *Early Childhood Education*. London: Paul Chapman Publishing.

Borton, H. (1963) *Do You Move as I Do?* London: Abelard-Schuman.

Brearley, M. (ed.) (1969) *Fundamentals in the First School*. Oxford: Blackwell.

Brierley, J. (1987) *Give Me a Child until He Is Seven*. London: The Falmer Press.

Brown, D. (1994) 'Play, the playground and the culture of children', in J. Moyles (ed.), *The Excellence of Play*. Milton Keynes: Open University Press.

Bruce, T. (1987) *Early Childhood Education*. London: Hodder and Stoughton.

Bruce, T. (1991) *Time to Play in Early Childhood Education*. London: Hodder and Stoughton.

Bruce, T. (1996) *Helping Young Children to Play*. London: Hodder and Stoughton.

Bruce, T. (1997) *Early Childhood Education* (2nd edn). London: Hodder and Stoughton.

Bruce, T. (2002) *Learning through Play: Babies, Toddlers and the Foundation Years*. London: Hodder and Stoughton.

Bruce, T. and Meggitt, C. (2002) *Childcare and Education*. (3rd edn) London: Hodder and Stoughton.

Bruner, J. (1968) *Towards a Theory of Instruction*. Cambridge, MA: Harvard University Press.

Calvin, W. (1997) *How Brains Think*. London: Weidenfeld and Nicholson.

Carnegie Corporation (1994) *Starting Points: Meeting the Needs of our Youngest Children*. New York: Carnegie Corporation.

Carter, R. (1998) *Mapping the Mind*. London: Orion.

David, T. (ed.) (1999) *Young Children Learning*. London: Paul Chapman Publishing.

Davies, M. (1976) 'An investigation into movement related to some aspects of cognitive development in young children'. PhD dissertation, University of London.

Davies, M. (1994) 'Good practice in dance' in *Dance Matters*. Spring, N. Carpenter, J. Meiners and J. Newman (eds). London: NDTA.

DES (1989) *Aspects of Primary Education: The Education of Children Under Five*. London: HMSO.

DES (1990) *Starting With Quality: The Report of Inquiry into the Quality of the Educational Experience Offered to 3 and 4 Year Olds*. London: HMSO.

DES (1992) *Physical Education in the National Curriculum*. London: HMSO.

DfEE and QCA (1999) *The National Curriculum: Handbook for Primary Teachers in England Key Stages 1 and 2*. London: HMSO.

Donaldson, M. (1978) *Children's Minds*. London: Fontana.

Dowling, M. (2000) *Young Children's Personal, Social and Emotional Development*. London: Paul Chapman Publishing.

Drummond, M.J. (1993) *Assessing Children's Learning*. London: David Fulton.

Edgington, M. (Lally, M.) (1998) *The Nursery Teacher in Action*. London: Paul Chapman Publishing.

Fisher, J. (1996) *Starting from the Child: Teaching and Learning from 4 to 8*. Buckingham: Open University Press.

Flemming, G. (1973) *Children's Dance*. Washington: American Association for Health, Physical Education and Recreation.

Gallahue, D. (1982) *Developmental Experiences for Children*. New York: Macmillan.

Gallahue, D. (1989) *Understanding Motor Development: Infants, Children, Adolescents*. Dubuque, IA: Brown and Benchmark (printers).

Gerhardt, L. (1973) *Moving and Knowing: The Young Child Orients Himself in Space*. Englewood Cliffs, NJ: Prentice-Hall.

Gopnik, A., Molzoff, A. and Kuhl, P. (1999) 'How babies think', in A. Gopnik, A. Molzaff and P. Kuhl, *The Science of Childhood*. London: Weidenfeld and Nicolson.

Gough, M. (1993) *In Touch with Dance*. Lancaster: Whitethorn Books.

Green Gilbert, A. (1992) *Creative Dance for All Ages*. Reston: The American Alliance for Health, Physical Education, Recreation and Dance.

Groves, L. (1989) 'Children with special needs', in A. Williams (ed.), *Issues in Physical Education for the Primary Years*. Lewes: Falmer Press.

Harlow, M. and Rolfe, L. (1992) *Let's Dance: A Handbook for Teachers*. London: BBC Educational.

Hawkins, A. (1964) *Creating through Dance*. Englewood Cliffs, NJ: Prentice-Hall.

Hinkley, C. (1980) *Creativity in Dance*. Australia: Sydney: Alternative Publishing Co-operative.

Hodgson, J. (2001) *Mastering Movement*. London: Methuen.

Holm, H. (1980) 'Hanya speaks', in J. Morrison Brown (ed.), *The Vision of Modern Dance*. London: Dance Books.

Hurst, V. (1994) 'Observing play in early childhood', in J. Moyles (ed.), *The Excellence of Play*. Milton Keynes: Open University Press.

Hutt, J.S., Tyler, S., Hutt, C. and Christopherson, H. (1988) *Play, Exploration and Learning: A Natural History of the Pre-school*. London: Routledge.

Ives, S.W. (1984) 'The development of expressivity in drawing', *British Journal of Educational Psychology*, 54: 152–9.

Jackson, L. (1993) *Childsplay: Movement Games for Fun and Fitness*. London: Thorsons.

Jamison, J. with Kaplan, H. (1993) *Dancing Spirit: An Autobiography*. New York: Doubleday.

Karstadt, L. and Medd, J. (2000) 'Children in the family and society', in R. Drury, L. Miller and R. Miller (eds), *Looking at Early Years Education and Care*. London: David Fulton.

Katz, L. and Chard, S. (1989) *Engaging Children's Minds. The Project Approach*. Norwood, NJ: Ablex.

Killingbeck, M. (1993) 'Participation – its relevance for appreciation'. M.Phil. dissertation, University of DeMontfort, Leicestershire.

Laban, R. (1948) *Modern Educational Dance*. London: MacDonald and Evans.

Laban, R. (1966) *Choreutics*. London: MacDonald and Evans.

Laban, R. (1980) *The Mastery of Movement*. (4th edn) London: MacDonald and Evans.

Laban, R. and Lawrence, F. (1947) *Effort*. London: MacDonald and Evans.

Lally, M. (1991) *The Nursery Teacher in Action*. London: Paul Chapman Publishing.

Lamb, W. (1965) *Posture and Gesture*. London: Gerald Duckworth.

Linfield, R. and Warwick, P. (1996) 'Assessment in the Early Years', in D. Whitebread (ed.), *Teaching and Learning in the Early Years*. London: Routledge.

Lowden, M. (1989) *Dancing to Learn*. London: Falmer Press.

Magill, R. (1998) *Motor Learning: Concepts and Applications*. New York: McGraw-Hill (International Edition).

Matthews, J. (1994) *Helping Children to Draw and Paint in Early Childhood*. London: Hodder and Stoughton.

Matthews, J. (2002) *Helping Children to Draw and Paint in Early Childhood* (2nd edn). London: Paul Chapman Publishing.

Maude, P. (1996) 'How do I do this better? From movement development into early years physical education', in D. Whitebread (ed.), *Teaching and Learning in the Early Years* (reprinted 2001). London: RoutledgeFalmer.

McPherson, B.D., Curtis, J.E. and Loy, J.W. (1989) *The Social Significance of Sport*. Champaign, Ill.: Human Kinetics Books.

Meadows, S. and Cashdan, A. (1988) *Helping Children Learn*. London: David Fulton.

Melville-Thomas, R. (1993) 'Moving, growing, learning: body movement behaviour in the development of the whole child', in *Focus on Dance Movement Therapy. Journal Two*. London: daCi UK.

Mosston, M. and Ashworth, S. (1994) *Teaching Physical Education*. New York: Macmillan College.

Moyles, J. (ed.) (1994) *The Excellence of Play*. Milton Keynes: Open University Press.

NAEYC (1992) *Developmentally Appropriate Practice in Early Childhood Programs. Serving: Children from Birth through 8* (2nd edn). Washington D.C.: National Association for the Education of Young Children.

NDTA (1998) *video: Teaching Dance in the Primary School*. London: NDTA with the support of the Arts Council.

Neisser, U. (1976) *Cognition and Reality*. San Francisco: W.H. Freeman.

Nielsen, L. (1992) *Space and Self*. Copenhagen: Sikon.

North, M. (1972) *Personality Assessment through Movement*. London: MacDonald and Evans.

Nutbrown, C. (1994) *Threads of Thinking*. London: Paul Chapman Publishing.

Peter, M. (1997) *Making Dance Special*. London: David Fulton.

Petricevic, B. (1991) 'Dance creativity and dance theatre', in S.W. Stinson (ed.), *Proceedings of the 1991 Conference of Dance and the Child*. Salt Lake City, UT: University of Utah.

Piaget, J. (1953) *The Origin of Intelligence in the Child*. London: Routledge and Kegan Paul.

Piaget, J. (1971) *Science of Education and the Psychology of the Child*. London: Longman.

Preston, V. (1963) *A Handbook for Modern Educational Dance*. London: MacDonald and Evans.

Preston-Dunlop, V. (1998) *Rudolf Laban: An Extraordinary Life*. London: Dance Books.

Pugh, G. and De'Ath, E. (1984) *The Needs of Parents*. London: Macmillan.

QCA (2000) *Curriculum Guidance for the Foundation Stage*. London: QCA.

QCA and DfEE (2000) *Physical Education: Teacher's Guide. Physical Education at Key Stages 1 and 2*. London: QCA.

Redfern, H.B. (1973) *Concepts in Modern Educational Dance*. London: Henry

Kimpton.

Roberts, M. and Tamburrini, J. (eds) (1981) *Child Development 0–5*. Edinburgh: Holmes McDougall.

Roberts, R. (2002) *Self Esteem and Early Learning*. London: Paul Chapman Publishing.

Roberton, M. and Halverson, L. (1984) *Developing Children – Their Changing Movement*. Philadelphia, PA: Lea and Febiger.

Rolfe, L. and Harlow, M. (1992) *Let's Dance: A Handbook for Teachers*. London: BBC Enterprises.

Russell, J. (1965) *Creative Dance in the Primary School*. London: MacDonald and Evans.

Schaffer, H. (1996) *Social Development*. Oxford: Blackwell.

Sherborne, V. (1990) *Developmental Movement for Children*. Cambridge: Cambridge University Press.

Singer, G. and Singer, J. (1990) *The House of Make Believe*. London: Harvard University Press.

Smith-Autard, J.M. (1994) *The Art of Dance in Education*. London: A. and C. Black.

Stinson, S.W. (1988) *Dance for Young Children: Finding the Magic in Movement*. Reston, VA: American Alliance for Health, Physical Education, Recreation and Dance.

Swanwick, K. (1982) 'The arts in education: dreaming or awake?' Special professorial lecture presented at the University of London, Institute of Education.

Thomas, J., Lee, A. and Thomas, K. (1988) *Physical Education for Children: Concepts into Practice*. Champaign Ill.: Human Kinetic Books.

Vygotsky, L.S. (1978) *Mind In Society: The Development of Higher Psychological Processes*. London: Harvard University Press.

Vygotsky, L.S. (1986) *Thought and Language*. London: MIT Press.

Wetton, P. (1988) *Physical Education in the Nursery and Infant School*. London: Croom Helm.

Whalley, M. (1994) *Learning to Be Strong: Setting Up a Neighbourhood Service for Under Fives and their Families*. London: Hodder and Stoughton.

Whitebread, D. (ed.) (1996) *Teaching and Learning in the Early Years*. London: Routledge. Reprinted (2001) RoutledgeFalmer.

Whitehead, M. (1990) *Language and Literacy in the Early Years*. London: Paul Chapman Publishing.

Whitehead, M. (2002) *Language and Literacy in the Early Years*. (2nd edn). London: Paul Chapman Publishing.

Williams, G. (1988) 'An attempt to define criteria for the effective teaching of dance in the primary school'. MA dissertation, University of Surrey.

Williams, G. (1991) 'Shaking, shivering and shuddering', in *Focus on Education. Journal One*. London: daCi UK.

Zaichkowsky, L.D., Zaichkowsky, L.B. and Martinek, T.J. (1980) *The Child and Physical Activity*. St Louis, MO: Mosby.

Index